Win and Win Again!

Win and Win Again!

Techniques for Playing Consistently Great Golf

CURTIS STRANGE

with Kenneth Van Kampen

CB

CONTEMPORARY
BOOKS

CHICAGO

Library of Congress Cataloging-in-Publication Data

Strange, Curtis.
    Win and win again : Curtis Strange's techniques for playing consistently great golf / Curtis Strange with Kenneth Van Kampen : foreword by Arnold Palmer.
       p.   cm.
    ISBN 0-8092-4322-9 (cloth)
        0-8092-4000-9 (paper)
     1. Golf.   2. Strange, Curtis.   3. Golfers—United States—
Biography.   I. Van Kampen, Kenneth.   II. Title.
GV965.S874   1990
796.352'092—dc20   89-77633
[B]   CIP

PHOTO CREDITS

All interior photos by Lawrence N. Levy, except as otherwise noted below.
All instructional illustrations by Ken Lewis.

Photos courtesy of AP/Wide World appear on pages xi, xvi, xviii, 57, and on color page 2 (bottom left and right). Photo courtesy of *Golf World* on page 44. Photos by Matthew Harris appear on pages 145, 196, 205, and on color page 2 (top). Photos by Leonard Kamsler appear on pages 45–47 (across the top), xix, 51–55, and 217. Photo by C. Ritchie on color page 3 (bottom). Photos on page 215 and color page 3 (top left) are from the Strange family collection. Photos by Mike Williams on pages xii and xiii. Photos courtesy of Wake Forest University on pages xiv and xv. Photo by F. Vuich on page 163.

Published by Contemporary Books, Inc.
Two Prudential Plaza, Chicago, Illinois 60601-6790
Manufactured in the United States of America
International Standard Book Number: 0-8092-4322-9 (cloth)
                                         0-8092-4000-9 (paper)

Quoted material on pages 173 and 181 is from *30 Exercises for Better Golf* by Dr. Frank W. Jobe, M.D. Copyright © 1986 Centinela Hospital Medical Center. Used by permission of Champion Press, Centinela Hospital Medical Center, 555 East Hardy Street, Inglewood, California 90301

*To Sarah, Thomas, and David,
who share my sacrifices and successes,
for their inspiration and support*

CONTENTS

Foreword

Perhaps there has been a touch of father in me in my friendship with Curtis Strange over the years. Not just because I am 25 years older than he is. More so, perhaps, because I knew his father well from our amateur days in the early 1950s, when I was living and working in Ohio after college before I turned pro. Tom Strange was a great guy. We got along very well, downed some suds together from time to time. We both became professionals, but Tom opted for club work, buying and operating a course at Virginia Beach, where he died when Curtis was just 14. I had pretty much lost track of Tom and his family as I embarked on and became immersed in my own tournament career. Then we began to hear about the golfing exploits of a young Virginia teenager named Curtis Strange, and before long my friends at Wake Forest, particularly the golf coach, Jesse Haddock, were proudly proclaiming that Curtis was entering Wake Forest on the Buddy Worsham Scholarship Fund program that I had established in memory of my college buddy and confidant who died in an auto accident while we were in school.

It didn't take long for Curtis to become the biggest star of the outstanding Wake Forest golf teams of that period in the mid-1970s and mark himself as a sure-pop future standout on the PGA Tour, which, of course, he has become in the 1980s. The clincher to that probability rating was the way he carried Wake Forest to the NCAA Championship and himself to the individual title with a clutch eagle on the 72nd hole that collected all the marbles by a single stroke. I have often thought, too, how my wife, Winnie, and I may have exerted some sort of parental influence on the new marriage of Curtis and Sarah Strange. He and I had an exhibition match booked right after their wedding, and they spent their honeymoon at our house.

I see some things that Curtis and I seem to have in common in our golf, in both our approaches to the game and the way we play it. We both hate to lose, and it shows on the course. It's certainly no secret that, just as Curtis has had to do, I had to learn to overcome flares of temper early in my career when things would happen that got in the way of victory. He and I are always determined to win.

That aside, Curtis impressed me early on with his intelligent approach and the steady intensity of his play from first tee to 18th green, even when he was not a serious contender. Who will forget how close he came to winning the 1985 Masters championship after starting the tournament with an 80? The mark of a winner: he never concedes defeat.

Curtis plays a pretty straightforward game. Although his style is quite different from mine, I like certain elements of his game a great deal. In my prime, I always fired at the pin, no matter where it was or where I was. There were times when I probably should have toned it down a bit, but that would have clashed with my natural aggressiveness. I have always played with the throttle wide open. On the other hand, Curtis Strange has the guts to take a chance yet the discipline to be patient and the intelligence to know when one or the other is the right approach. He's willing to wait for scoring opportunities instead of forcing them, although he gets many such chances because of his superior shotmaking. He knows the mechanics of his swing inside and out, and this knowledge certainly helps him work the ball so well. The fact that he is such a fine student of the game well qualifies him to teach the amateur player how to get the most out of his or her golf.

Even before his marvelous feat of winning the U.S. Open Championship in the successive years of 1988 and 1989, Curtis was considered in many quarters to be America's best player of the time and one of the world's two or three finest pros. But those stirring victories at The Country Club and Oak Hill dissolved the pressure to put a major title on his record, which had been building on the tour for the better part of a decade. Nobody was more pleased than I when Curtis won the first Open in the grueling play-off against Nick Faldo; and it was a delight when, a few weeks later, Winnie and I had dinner with Curtis and Sarah and shared his happiness, something only another pro who has been there can really appreciate. We got together, the four of us, not long after Oak Hill, and I suspect there will be similar occasions in the years to come.

—Arnold Palmer
October 1989

Introduction

I guess I was luckier than the average person when it came to my start in golf. First, my father, Tom Strange, was a golf professional and a darned good player, too, so I always had a good example to copy and learn from by watching. Dad laid the groundwork for the game I have today by teaching me early the right way to grip a club and stand up to the ball. The fundamentals he taught me are the same ones I use today. Besides the physical aspects of swinging a club, Dad also taught me to believe in myself and never to say "I can't do it," a feeling I still carry with me today.

Another reason I was lucky was because my twin brother, Allan, was (and still is) as competitive as I am. Whether it was golf, baseball, football, or fishing, we were always trying to outdo each other, and that competitive experience was crucial to my development into a tour-caliber player.

Allan and I were just like any kids who loved the game—we couldn't get enough playing time in during golf season. I can remember watching many a professional tournament on television when I was young and not being able to sit through the whole thing because I'd get so fired up by what I saw that I'd have to go out and play. Arnold Palmer was my idol, and it wouldn't take long watching in front of the set before I was out on the practice green pretending I was him, charging a birdie putt home on 18 for a one-stroke victory. (In the press conference following the U.S. Open play-off I mentioned that winning that title gave me the hope that somewhere a kid might be practicing and imagining the same things I once did, only he might be pretending he was Curtis Strange.) Right there is another example of what Dad did for me—since he was in the golf business, we could pretty much play whenever we wanted to, and that chance, as you might imagine, was as important to my becoming a professional golfer as anything. My desire to be a touring player from the time I was very young drove me to take full advantage of that

My father, Tom, tees off in a second-round match of the 1955 U.S. Amateur Championship.

opportunity. So, like most touring pros who got started in the game young and got to where they are through a lot of practice, I was no exception.

There were also a lot of other kids around to play against, but Allan was always my toughest competition. He developed into a pretty good player himself and played a year (1981) on tour before dropping out and getting a "real" job as a stockbroker. I think part of the reason I've had more success at golf is because I worked harder at it when we were kids. When spring and summer rolled around, Allan spent more time playing baseball and then football in the fall. Not that I didn't enjoy other sports—I did, but I preferred to devote most of my time to golf. I guess our experiences in Little League baseball illustrate as well as anything our preferences. When we were 11, Allan was chosen to play in the league all-star game. The game date happened to fall on the same day as the Virginia State Junior Golf Championship. Faced with that choice, Allan decided to play in the baseball game instead of the tournament. The following year, I was picked to play in the all-star game and had to make the same decision. It was no contest—I wanted to play golf. Ironically, I've always thought that Allan chose the wrong sport when he went into profes-

In front, from left to right, are my mother, Nancy; me; my twin brother, Allan; sister, Anne; and father, Tom. Standing behind us are my grandparents.

Chandler Harper, a great friend and teacher, keeps an eye on my swing between rounds of the 1973 Eastern Amateur Championship.

sional golf. I honestly believe that his potential in baseball was limitless and that if he'd stuck with it past high school, making it to the major leagues would have been within his reach.

When I was 14, my father died of cancer. Sadly, he had just realized a longtime dream of owning and running a golf course, the White Sands Country Club, in Virginia Beach. After Dad was gone, there were financial problems, and our family lost the course. My mother, Nancy, went back to work and raised my brother, my sister, Anne, and me by herself. Probably the best thing that happened to me after that was meeting Chandler Harper when I was 15. Chandler, a member of the PGA Hall of Fame, was a friend of my father and had compiled a fine amateur and professional record, winning a number of tournaments, including the 1950 PGA Championship, while never competing full-time on tour. When we met he was, and still is, owner and head professional at the Bide-A-Wee Country Club, in Portsmouth, Virginia.

Chandler recognized that I had good fundamentals and the potential to be a decent player. But he also noticed that, since I was a kid, I could easily fall into bad habits. He has an excellent eye for the little things that can go wrong in a golf swing and helped me fix mine when it went bad and kept me on track. An example of this was when, soon after we became friends, Chandler made a minor adjustment in my grip and advised me to keep my right leg firmer on the backswing. Three weeks later I won the Virginia State Junior Cham-

Good friend and fellow tour player Jay Haas and I mug for the camera during our collegiate playing days at Wake Forest.

pionship. I've always been the determined type who's worked hard for the things I've wanted, and with that characteristic comes a tendency sometimes to get angry and be hard on myself. Chandler saw that but never scolded me for it. He knew that that kind of fire was important to being a good competitor. From the time I met Chandler to the time I turned pro, I was always recognized as a member at Bide-A-Wee. To this day he and I have remained close friends—his guidance meant a lot to me after my dad passed away.

The next big tournament I won was the Southeastern Amateur in 1973. Then that fall I started my first year at Wake Forest. The Deacons were well known in our part of the country, and it was a dream of mine to play for them, as Jay Sigel, Lanny Wadkins, and Arnold Palmer had. To my amazement, I was awarded the scholarship given in Arnold's name. I couldn't have been more proud, and I didn't even bother talking to any other schools.

Playing on the golf team at Wake Forest meant a lot to me, since it was the alma mater of so many good players, deep in tradition, and a good stepping-stone to the pros. Besides Wake's reputation for having fine players, it also had an excellent coach, Jesse Haddock, who was a friend of my father.

As it turned out, my freshman golf season was something most kids dream about. I played in the number-two spot behind Jay Haas, a good friend and now fellow tour pro, who was a year ahead of me. In the NCAA Championship, I came to the final tee of the par-five finishing hole needing eagle to nail down both the team and individual titles. I hit a good drive, followed it with a 1-iron to eight feet, then rolled in the putt. It was a very emotional victory for both me and the team, because it was the first NCAA Team title for Wake and Coach Haddock. Looking back, I have to admit that what I had done, both individually and as part of the team, didn't really sink in at the time, since I was just an 18-year-old freshman and hadn't fully realized exactly what had been accomplished. To top all that off, I received another thrill—being named NCAA College Player of the Year. Although all of that is well behind me now, I'll always be proud of my team and individual achievements of 1974.

Up to that point I had continued to harbor the goal of someday playing golf for a living. And though my record as an amateur was pretty good, there was always that little bit of doubt rattling its chain in the back of my mind. But after all that had happened during my freshman year, I really started to believe that I might be able to make it as a touring pro.

The following year was an important one for me, for a couple of reasons. First, I met my future wife, Sarah, at a fraternity party. She was attending a local all-girls school, Salem College. Meeting and then later marrying Sarah were the two greatest things that ever happened to me—I wouldn't be where I am today if it hadn't been for her positive influence and confidence in me.

Second, I started to get the same itch in the classroom that I used to get when I was a kid watching golf on TV: I wanted to get out and try my luck at playing for a living. Despite this I tried to be patient, and I waited until after my junior year before deciding to leave college and turn professional.

Now, I can't finish talking about college without again mentioning my golf coach, Jesse Haddock. He did the things a good coach should have done by keeping me in line and instilling some discipline in me when I needed it both on and off the course. I can remember at the time thinking that Coach Haddock was being too tough on me, but, looking back, I realize it was for my own good. Like Chandler, he recognized what might be in my future, and he wanted me to give 100 percent toward seeing it through. Coach realized that my best quality as a player was my "never give up" attitude, which he helped teach me to channel positively. He saw that sometimes I had to get mad to bring out the best in myself, and he didn't try to change that; once he said that I was the only player he'd ever coached who "played best when he was mad."

NCAA champs! This team picture was taken immediately after Wake Forest was victorious in 1974. From left to right are: Jay Haas, Lex Alexander, Bill Argabrite, me, Coach Jesse Haddock, Bob Byman, and David Thore.

The day I left school I took my first step toward a pro career by signing a contract with International Management Group, which has managed me ever since. It was my first business decision, and one of the best moves I've ever made. Hughes Norton of IMG has always treated me as an individual, not a commodity or business interest. IMG never failed to be supportive through the ups and downs of the last 13 years, and, believe me, there *were* some downs.

Everything started out rosy the summer of 1976 after I left school. My plan was to head overseas and get some competitive experience (and hopefully put some money in the bank), get married in the fall before the tour-qualifying school was held, then start my rookie year on the U.S. Tour the following January. As it turned out, my foreign excursion went successfully, since I played pretty well and was basically satisfied with my performance. Then Sarah and I got married in September, right on schedule. But what neither of us had planned on was my failing the tour school. That possibility hadn't really crossed my mind, but I bogeyed the last three holes in the final round to miss by a shot. The disappointment of having finished poorly and then coming up just short was awful—I felt as if I had failed for the first time at something that really mattered. I remember doubting myself, wondering if I really had what it took to play in the tour if that was the best I could do. Sarah and I were both in tears as we drove back to the hotel, trying to decide whether it was worth it for me to try to qualify again or whether I should figure out something else to do for a living. As she later put it, here we had put all our apples in one cart, only to have the wheels fall off. That night we talked it over and decided I'd come too close not to try it one more time. That was back when the PGA held two qualifying schools each year, in the fall and in the spring.

Once that decision was made, my outlook changed from dismal to determined, thanks to Sarah's support and a positive attitude. I made up my mind that there wasn't going to have to be a third time; I was going to get my card at the following spring school.

To get ready for it, I decided to head back across the Atlantic, this time taking Sarah with me, so I could stay sharp by competing in some tournaments over in Europe. IMG helped by taking care of our arrangements and convincing some of the sponsors to pay our expenses. My main concern was to play—the more the better.

Overall, I was encouraged with my performance that winter in Europe. Even though I made some money, things were pretty lean for us. When we got back home we lived in a summer house in North Carolina owned by Sarah's parents, while I continued to practice and play, play and practice, to get ready for the upcoming school. It was

Third round, 1979 Pensacola Open: Despite the serious expression, I shot 63 en route to winning my first professional tournament.

held that spring in Pinehurst at the No. 2 Course, which happens to be my favorite. As it turned out, I was indeed ready this time, and I earned my card easily.

That was one very big hurdle behind me, though I knew there were tougher ones ahead. Having a card allows you to compete on tour, but it's no guarantee you'll make it out there. Every year there are a number of guys who lose their cards because they don't perform well enough, and that's something every rookie worries about. Fortunately, I never came very close to losing mine, but I didn't exactly set the circuit on fire my first few years. I concentrated mainly on improving my game in the first year, though I did come close to winning in Hartford and in Pensacola. I wasn't dissatisfied with the season outcome: 87th on the money list, with $28,144.

The next year I came closer to winning but finished about the same: 88th in the money, with $29,346 in earnings. Sarah had been traveling with me since the start, and back then the cost for two people to stay on the road with the tour was about $30,000 a year, so we were just about breaking even. Despite that, our hopes remained high.

The breakthrough came the next year, when I won my first tournament, at Pensacola. There was nothing too fancy about it except for a hot third round, but it was my first win, which is something that's a lot more important than one might think. What made it even better was that Sarah's parents were down there with us, so we topped it off with a big victory party. Winning Pensacola boosted me into the top 60 money winners—I finished 21st, with $138,368. But more important, it got me over another hurdle—I had proved to myself that not only could I compete on tour, I could *win* on tour.

Of course, one title doesn't qualify you as a great player or guarantee that you'll win again. In fact, at the start of the 1980 season my game took a turn for the worse. Soon after that I met and started working with a noted teacher named Jimmy Ballard. Jimmy taught the swing method (passed on to him by former tour pro Sam Byrd), that is referred to as "connection," which I'll talk more about later. My game took a turn for the better, and I had a great year, winning twice and finishing third in the money. Over the next four years I finished 9th, 10th, 21st, and 14th, consecutively, and in doing so I got over another hurdle—being a consistent money winner.

In 1985 I had my best year; ironically, it was also my most disappointing time on tour up to then. To that point I had continued to prove myself to be a solid player by making a good living and winning five tournaments. Personally, I'm not the type of guy who tells the world of his goals, but each year I know down deep what I

Attempting to blast out of Rae's Creek on number 13, Sunday, at the 1985 Masters. I bogeyed the hole, then eventually finished two strokes behind winner Bernhard Langer.

want to achieve. It was about at that point that I really started to gear myself up for the major championships, because as every professional golfer knows, the major titles are what pro golf is all about.

Through 1984 my record in the majors was nothing to write home about, as my best finish had been third place in the U.S. Open that year. It didn't appear it would improve any at the start of the 1985 Masters after I opened with 80. I wasn't about to give up, however, especially since I really hadn't played that badly; but an 80 being an 80, I assumed I'd probably miss the cut, so I went ahead and made plane reservations to go home Friday night. Those were quickly canceled the next afternoon after a 65 qualified me to complete the tournament. A 68 in the third round put me in the thick of things, a stroke behind leader Raymond Floyd. On Sunday, after four birdies in the first nine holes, I had a four-shot lead over Bernhard Langer.

Unfortunately, this is where the old sayings "It wasn't meant to be" and "You can't win 'em all" (although I really don't believe in them) painfully come in. On the homeward nine I went for the green in two on the par-five 13th and 15th holes and found water hazards both times. Instead of two birdies, I made two bogeys and eventually ended up in a tie for second with Floyd and Seve Ballesteros, two shots behind the winner, Langer.

That was a tough loss to take and by far the biggest disappointment of my career up to then, but there were some positive aspects to it. I realized that, like my near miss in the 1976 tour school, if I could come that close to winning a major tournament, then I actually had it in me to win. Besides, just flirting with victory in a major tournament had given me enough of a taste of it to realize how badly I wanted one.

Despite what happened at the Masters, 1985 was a good year, as I won three tournaments and led the money list for the first time. I slipped down to 32nd in 1986, though I won once, then bounced back to top the list again in 1987 after winning three times that year. After that, murmurs started about when I was going to win a major, and though I didn't think I had a monkey on my back, I was feeling some pressure. That's why when I won the 1988 U.S. Open at The Country Club in Brookline, Massachusetts, it couldn't have come at a better time. It was one more hurdle, and when the final putt dropped to seal the play-off win over Nick Faldo, it was the greatest feeling I'd ever had. But that accomplishment doesn't belong only to me, but rather to all the people who've supported and been behind me since my start in golf. And I don't look at that last "major" hurdle as the end of something, but hopefully as the beginning of more good things to come.

Final round, '89 U.S. Open: reacting to a 15-foot birdie putt that dropped on the sixteenth hole; giving me a two-shot lead with two holes to play.

Curtis Strange
May 1989

———————————●
▼

I hadn't expected to need to add a postscript to the introduction before this book was published, but being fortunate enough to win the U.S. Open a second time in 1989 makes me honored to do so.

Throughout 1988 the Open trophy had been on display at the Kingsmill Country Club near my home in Kingsmill, Virginia. The week before the 1989 tournament it was packed up and sent back to the United States Golf Association in Far Hills, New Jersey, and I hated to see it go. Little did I know it would be coming back so soon. I can't say I expected to win at Oak Hill, since my game hadn't been too sharp up to that point in the year (although I had chalked up a couple of second-place finishes). Besides, I don't go into any tournament "expecting" to win; I just hope to make as good a showing as I can, though I will admit that I was more determined than usual to play well, since the last thing I wanted to do as last year's champ was to miss the cut or finish way out of it. The four rounds I played proved what a crazy, up-and-down game golf can be, as well as the importance of using one's head and sticking to strategy.

The first day, Thursday, I just wanted to shoot a decent score and avoid making a really high number that would be tough to make up for. I ended up posting a 71, one over par, putting me five shots in back of Payne Stewart, Jay Don Blake, and Bernhard Langer, each of whom shot 66.

On day two I had one of those wondrous rounds in which you feel you can do no wrong. Nearly every shot was square and in the direction I intended, and the putter felt great in my hands. The result was a six-under 64 and a one-shot lead over Tom Kite.

Despite how easy the game seemed on Friday, though, it suddenly got a lot harder for the third round on Saturday, as is the nature of golf. My swing and putting stroke just didn't feel as good as the day before, and the tough layout landed a couple of counterpunches as I settled for a three-over 73, putting me three behind the leader, Kite. That night I stayed on the practice range till dark, not trying to detect any flaws in my swing, but just hitting balls in an effort to find a pattern in the shots.

The next day, Sunday, I felt a little more confident about my ball-striking after warming up on the range. My putting touch, however, was cold on the practice green. Being only three shots back, my game plan was to concentrate on keeping the ball out of trouble and not to shoot myself out of it in the early going. My goal was to be patient and make pars; if birdies happened, okay, but above all I wanted to steer clear of bogeys and worse. As it turned out, my strategy paid off. I missed only four greens, finishing on the fringe three out of those four times, en route to parring the first 15 holes. Meanwhile, the leaders faltered and fell behind. Through the 15th hole I hadn't really hit any approach shots close to the hole and my putting feel hadn't improved, so most of the day I concentrated mainly on getting the first putt close and avoiding any knee knockers for par. Finally, on 16, a 439-yard par four, I drove in the fairway and followed with a 6-iron to 15 feet. At that point I had gone 35 holes without a birdie, but I held a one-shot lead over Ian Woosnam, Chip Beck, and Mark

McCumber. Of all the putts I'd faced that day, this was the one I wanted most. I read it to be pretty straight, then stroked it into the center of the hole. Of all the 278 shots I took from Thursday through Sunday, that was the most important. Now I had a two-shot lead going to 17, a 458-yard par four that I had yet to score better than bogey on. This time I split the fairway, hit the fat of the green with a 3-iron, and two-putted for four. One more hole to play—"four more swings." I told myself, *Let's not do anything stupid or fancy, just make par.* A good drive put me in the fairway, leaving another 6-iron to the green. I hit it solid, but it carried a little too far: the 18th green at Oak Hill slopes from back to front, and that day the pin was toward the front on the right. Though I didn't want to have a long, fast, downhill putt, my approach landed on the back of the green. After getting to the green and surveying the situation, I realized that under no circumstance did I want to leave my first putt short of the cup, since that would leave a tricky downhiller for par that might easily slide well past and lead to a four-putt. *No hero stuff,* I thought, *just get this one past the cup and take two putts coming back if you have to.* The first putt rolled down the slope and stopped 10 feet past; the next one stopped just short, and I tapped in for bogey. The only player who could catch me now was Scott Simpson, who was playing in the next and final group. Scott needed an eagle on 18 to tie, but he drove in the right rough and was short of the green with his second shot. I had won again. Though nothing could compare to the thrill of winning at The Country Club, this came pretty close. Reflecting on it, I take a great deal of pride in the fact that the last person to win two Opens in a row was Ben Hogan in 1950-1951, and even more pride in view of the many great players who haven't successfully defended the title.

I have to admit that all of this didn't immediately sink in. All I knew as I posed with the trophy for the legion of photographers that had dutifully tramped through the muddy sidelines (the tournament had been plagued with rain and soggy conditions) throughout the week was that I was darned glad to be bringing that big silver cup back to Kingsmill again.

Curtis Strange
July 1989

Win and Win Again!

1
THE REASONS I WROTE
THIS BOOK

I've played in at least two dozen pro-ams each year since I joined the tour in 1978, so I've had plenty of opportunity to observe the games of "average" amateurs. For me, it's frustrating to see a player who I can see has the potential to play a good game, but is unfortunately lacking certain elements. If I can I'll try to help a person out with a tip or two if I don't think it will confuse him, but most of the time I know he would benefit more from in-depth instruction, which is impossible for me to give during the course of a competition. Besides, playing golf and teaching golf are two very different things, and I'm the first to admit that I don't have a particularly good eye for rooting out minute swing faults the way some people do.

My personal fundamentals for the long and short game will help the average amateur reach his or her scoring potential.

Despite that, I believe I can teach my own personal fundamentals for the long and short game and help the average amateur reach his or her scoring potential by helping him or her understand the strategic aspects of the game. So when it was proposed to me that I write an instruction book, I jumped at the chance, because through it I might be able to help recreational players enjoy golf more, which is what the game is all about.

I'm not saying that a book is a substitute for the hands-on instruction and expertise of a qualified teaching pro. I owe much of my success to those who have taught and guided me. But I also read and learned from golf books when I was young, which added to my knowledge of the game. (In fact, even at this point in my career I'm continually learning more things about golf, and I feel as if I've never stopped learning about it.) Now I'd like to give someone else the same thing I got from books. My hope is to convey what I've learned about golf, through my amateur and professional experiences, to the person who plays for fun, be it a high handicapper or low handicapper, senior or junior, male or female. Bear in mind, though, that what you find in this book may differ from what you've read, heard, or been taught elsewhere, because this is golf as I perceive it and play it, and my way is certainly not the only way.

A BRIEF WORD ABOUT "CONNECTION"

As I mentioned in the Introduction, there are three people who've had a major influence on the way I swing a golf club: first my father, who taught me the basics I still use today; next, Chandler Harper, who helped keep me on track and smoothed out the rough edges when I was a teenager, when I could easily have strayed into bad habits; and finally, Jimmy Ballard, whose "connection" theory has influenced my swing thoughts in recent years.

To hold a heavy object such as a shag bag filled with golf balls, you instinctively spread your feet, flex your knees, bend at the waist, and keep your upper arms close—or "connected"—to your chest.

To heave the bag forward, the natural move is to store energy by shifting your weight to your right side and coiling the big muscles in the back and chest.

Very simply, the main premise of connection is that to swing a golf club correctly, you have to use your whole body, not just certain parts of it. The big muscles of your legs and upper body and the smaller muscles of your arms and hands all have to play a part in swinging a golf club, and they all have to work in proper conjunction with one another—"connected" with one another. If disconnection occurs, then you won't make the most efficient use of your body and thus won't play up to your potential.

The beauty of the connection theory is that it isn't something

Then use the power of your big muscles by shifting your weight left, driving with your legs, and uncoiling your upper body.

If the throw was a good one, your weight ends up on your left side and your hands extend toward the target. Note how each of these photos resembles different positions found in a good golf swing.

you really have to learn, because we all know how to do it instinctively. For example: Suppose you had a heavy object, like a large shag bag filled with golf balls, and were told to throw it underhand as far as you could. To do that, you wouldn't use just your arms. To heave it as far as possible, you'd incorporate everything—legs, trunk, arms—into the motion probably without even thinking about it, because you'd want to expend maximum energy/force into tossing the bag.

Just as the big muscles of the body play a major role in lifting, moving, or heaving a heavy object, so should they in swinging a golf club. However, because a golf club is a relatively light object, there is a tendency to overuse the small, quick muscles of the arms and hands while swinging. The trick is to make them work in connection with the larger muscles of the legs and upper body; all work together to swing the club back and return it squarely and briskly to the ball.

Connection begins at address, before any motion is made. Think back to the heavy shag bag: The first thing you'd do before trying to throw it would be to settle into a "ready" position, a position that would be most conducive to performing the throw. You'd bend your arms a little at the elbows and bring them into your body, spread your feet for balance, brace your knees slightly inward, and bend a little at the hips, getting your muscles ready to spring. The same applies to the golf swing—if you don't set up connected, you won't swing connected.

I'll warn you right here that the connection method breaks a couple of classic swing rules, rules that I refer to as "swing myths," which will be described in Chapter 3. You'll be a better golfer for breaking them—I know I am. As far as I'm concerned, the word *connection* means everything in regard to the swing. Ever since I started playing, I've always been open to experimenting and trying different methods, and I had my own ideas about how to best strike a golf ball. Then I found that connection made sense and helped me to tie together the swing thoughts that I'd had kicking around in my head for a long time. For the first time I really felt like I understood my own golf swing. And once you understand your swing, you've already got a big part of the battle won. And trust me, if you pay attention, I promise that you'll gain an understanding of the method behind this madness and be able to make it work for you! Another part of the beauty of connection is that it will work for anyone, whether you're a tour pro who's been playing for years or a casual player just trying to build a reliable swing for Sunday afternoon.

PRO-AM

"Pro-am" is short for the words *professional* and *amateur* and is the term for a tournament in which teams of one pro and usually three amateurs compete in medal play. Amateurs play net, with full handicap; lowest single score per hole goes on the card. The pro-am is a regular part of most tour events (except majors) and is usually held on Wednesdays. Any amateur is eligible to apply for a playing slot, but the entrance fee is usually high—between $2,000 and $5,000 depending on the tournament—the proceeds of which go to charity and toward part of the purse. I like playing in pro-ams because it gives me the chance to meet a lot of nice people, plus it's a good feeling to know that some of the money raised is going to a good cause.

2
THE BASICS

I mentioned earlier that my father taught me the basics of the golf swing, which I still use today. In this chapter I'll pass them on to you—how to hold the club properly and how to stand up to the ball and put your body in the correct position to make a good swing. The basics are the foundation of the swing. Just as there's no way you'll be able to build a decent house on a poor foundation, neither will you be able to build a decent golf swing without the proper fundamentals.

I want to stress here that if you're helping a junior learn the game, take care to teach him or her the basics correctly. Just as good habits are more easily picked up at a young age, so are bad ones. I know I'm grateful to both my father and Chandler Harper for starting me out correctly and making sure I stayed that way. You can do the same favor for a child by keeping an eye on him or her to make sure that good fundamentals are adhered to.

GRIP

Don't make the mistake of thinking you can simply slap your hands on the club in whatever way feels comfortable. There's a right and wrong way to do everything, and the right grip is essential to getting proper hand and wrist action. Your hands are your only link to the golf club; if you don't learn how to grip correctly, you'll just make things harder on yourself.

Start with the left hand. Open it and lay the club diagonally across your fingers so that when you close your hand, the butt end of the club is wedged firmly against the heel pad and the thumb lies on the top, just right of center. Next, put your right hand on the club so the lifeline on the palm lies directly on top of your left thumb and the club is cradled in your right finger joints. The right thumb should lie just off center. The palms should be parallel—facing each other.

The butt end of the club should be wedged firmly against the heel pad of the left hand.

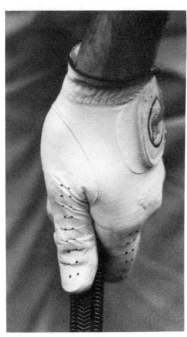

The left thumb should be just right of center.

The back of your left hand should face the target. Use a mirror to make sure your left hand looks like this.

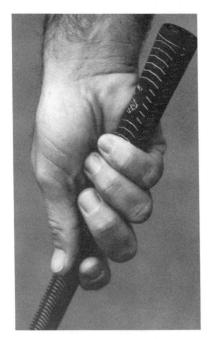

The club should be cradled in the fingers of the right hand.

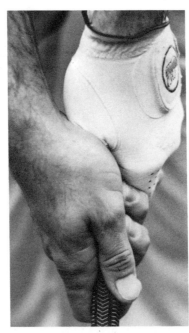

Make sure the lifeline on the right palm is pressed firmly on top of your left thumb, with the right thumb just left of center.

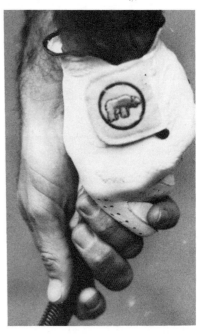

Fingers should be snug against one another without spaces between them. But I do extend my right index finger slightly so a small gap forms between it and my right middle finger.

Palms should be parallel.

The three points between your hands and shoulders will naturally form a triangle.

Look in a mirror and observe how the points of your hands and shoulders form a triangular shape. I'll be referring to this triangle later.

Types of Grips

Your hands should work together as a single unit, not separately. How you "link" them together determines the type of grip you take. There are three types: interlocking, overlapping (also known as the Vardon grip), and the 10-finger grip.

I use the overlap, which is the most popular among tour players and golfers in general. To take it, lay the little finger of your right hand into the valley formed between the index and second finger of your left hand, butting your right ring finger firmly against your left index finger.

To take the interlock, weave the right little finger together with your left index finger, so the tip of your right little finger lies between the first two knuckles of your left hand and the tip of your left index finger lies between the last two knuckles of your right hand. This method is favorable for players with short fingers, who may find the overlapping grip difficult or uncomfortable.

The advantage of these two methods is that they physically bond your hands together, helping them work as a single unit. But if neither hold is comfortable (and the way you hold the club should feel comfortable to you), you may want to try the 10-finger grip by butting your right little finger against your left index finger, as you would when holding a baseball bat. Kids may find it easier to hold the club this way when learning. By all means, don't be embarrassed to use this method if you like it. A good friend of mine, Bob Rosburg, used it to win the 1959 PGA. Former Masters champ and current senior tour player Art Wall uses it, as well as one of my peers on tour, Dave Barr.

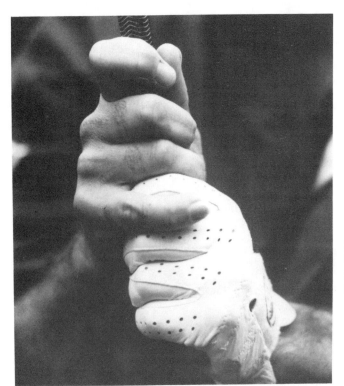

I prefer the overlapping grip, with the little finger of the right hand lying in the valley formed between the index and middle fingers of the left hand.

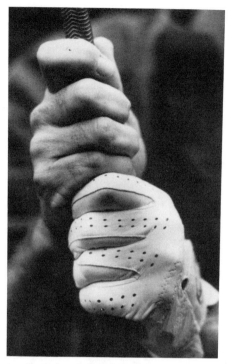

To take an interlocking grip, weave the little finger of your right hand with the left index finger.

Another way to hold the club is with the 10-finger grip, with the right little finger butting firmly against the left index finger.

Grip Position

Grip position is crucial. Position is determined by where the *V*s formed by the thumb and index finger of each hand point. There's an area between your nose and right shoulder that I call the "safety zone," meaning your position is okay as long as the *V*s point somewhere between the two points. If the *V*s are more toward your nose, your position is considered weak; if they are more toward your right shoulder, it's considered strong. There isn't any specific position that's better than another. Johnny Miller has had a very successful career using a weak grip. Paul Azinger, the 1987 PGA Player of the Year, and Billy Casper both grip the club in a very strong position. However, gripping in an overly weak or strong position will force you to make certain adjustments to compensate. I suggest starting out neutral and making adjustments from there if your shots aren't flying as straight as you'd like. A good idea is to forget about your hands and check your forearm position instead. If your forearms are parallel to your target line, then your hand position will automatically be okay.

If your hand position is poor, be aware that it's a tough habit to

The "safety zone" is between your nose and right shoulder. If the Vs of both hands point somewhere between the two points, your grip position is okay.

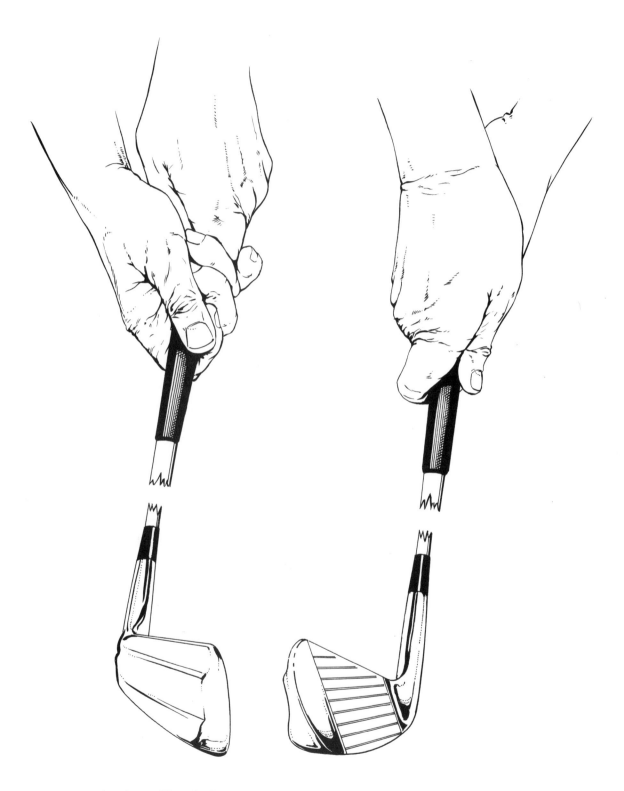

A grip position that's too strong (left) may result in the clubface being closed at impact, while a weak grip (right) may result in an open clubface.

break, since the main feedback you get from the club is through your hands—altering their position on the club will change the way the clubhead feels as you swing it from start to finish. Getting your hands into an acceptable position is necessary, however, because otherwise, as previously mentioned, you'll have to make compensations in your downswing in order to square the club to the ball.

When proper hand and wrist action occurs, the right hand passes over the left through impact, squaring the clubface to the ball—this is known as "releasing" the hands. If your shots are starting out

Always go back to the basics when trouble arises.

If your forearms are approximately level with each other at address, your grip position should be sound.

straight and then curving too much to the right, it means the clubface is open at impact and could be an indication that you need to strengthen your grip position so you can close the clubface sooner on the downswing. If shots are starting to curve too far left, it's because you're closing the clubface before impact, and your grip position may need to be weakened. I say "could be" and "may" in both of these cases because poor grip position is not always the cause of crooked shots, but it's a good place to start investigating. Remember, always go back to the basics first when trouble arises.

If your right forearm is below your left, grip position will be too strong.

If your right forearm is above your left, then grip position will be too weak.

Everyone's Grip Is a Little Different

A closing note on grip. Because everyone's hands and fingers are different sizes, lengths, and thicknesses, and because grip position varies from player to player, everyone's grip is going to look a little different. That's okay. Just remember that the function of every grip should be to place the hands comfortably on the club so they can work together as a unit throughout the swing.

ADDRESS

Now that you know how to hold the club, you've got to know how to stand up to the ball, or "address" it. Getting into proper position isn't difficult. Start with a 5-iron and simply stand up straight: feet, knees, hips, and shoulders parallel. Spread your feet wide, about shoulder

Proper foot position is crucial: The right foot should be square to the target line; the left foot should be turned outward (to the left).

For proper posture and correct distance from the ball, stand up straight with your feet spread shoulder width and arms extended in front of you; then flex slightly at the knees.

Next, bend slowly at the waist, keeping your arms firm.

Continue bending at the waist until the sole of the club rests flat against the ground.

width; then flex a little at the knees, "knocking" them inward slightly, so the kneecaps feel as if they're directly above the insteps of your feet. The knees should feel active and springlike, but make sure to flex them just a little instead of out-and-out bending them. The left foot should be turned outward slightly to the left, while the right foot remains square (at a 90-degree angle) or turned out just a hair. Next, hold the club straight out in front of you; then slowly bend at the waist, keeping your back straight, until the clubhead rests on the ground.

Your posture depends mostly on your height and build. Taller, slimmer people will naturally stand closer to the ball and thus should crouch a little more. Shorter people, who must stand farther from the ball, should stand a little taller. Whichever extreme you lean toward, if you pass the following test, your posture is okay: 1. knees are flexed enough so kneecaps are directly above the arches of your feet; 2. back is straight and there's enough bend at the waist to allow the arms to hang down relaxed, left hand at least four inches from the inside of the left thigh.

Arms

Your arms should hang relaxed from your shoulders so the bottom point of your "triangle" points directly at the ball. (With a 5-iron, ball position should be just forward of center. I'll talk more later on about where the ball should be with the different clubs.) In other words, your hands should be even with the ball. A lot of instruction prescribes setting the hands ahead of the ball so a straight line is formed by the left arm and clubshaft from the clubhead to the left shoulder, but I think that this sets up a poor angle that, besides feeling unnatural, usually results in blocked hand action at impact. The correct angle is formed when the hands are even with the ball and you have a perfect triangle that points at the ball.

The upper parts of your arms should brush lightly against your chest. There, it's connected—if it's held away from the chest, you're starting out disconnected before you begin the swing. That's one of the reasons why players who stand too far from the ball make disconnected swings—they're bent over too much from the waist, weight is on the toes, and the back of the upper arms is completely disconnected away from the chest, or "out of the sockets."

At address, make sure that feet, knees, hips, and shoulders are parallel;
knees are "knocked" inward slightly.

Posture will be good if: 1) knees are flexed so the kneecaps are above the arches of the feet; and 2) back is straight and the arms hang freely, left hand at least four inches from the left thigh.

Weight Distribution

Weight should be evenly distributed between the left foot and right foot, and slightly forward on the balls of your feet. You should feel balanced and comfortable, and in a position that I can only describe as "athletically ready." It's very similar to an infielder waiting for the batter to make contact or a tennis player anticipating a serve—both putting their bodies into a position from which it will be easy to spring into action.

A good test for finding out whether your posture is good and your weight distribution is correct is to have a friend give you a gentle push, first from the front, then from the back. If you're easily knocked off balance, it's a sign that you're standing too straight, causing your center of gravity to be too high. (Most cases of poor weight distribution stem from too much weight either forward, on the toes, or back, on the heels.) To lower your center of gravity, bend gradually at the knees and waist until a little shove doesn't knock you off your feet. Next, have your friend push you from the left side, then from the right side. Again, if you lose balance, it's a sign either that your weight is too much to one side and should be redistributed more equally, or that your feet aren't wide enough apart—make sure they're spread as far apart as your shoulders are wide.

Make sure your feet are spread as far apart as your shoulders are wide.

3
THE BIG-MUSCLE SWING

In Chapter 1 I said I believed there were certain "rules" about the swing that were actually fallacies. I believe that if you write off those fallacies, you'll take the first step to learning a better way to strike a golf ball.

The key to scoring well in golf is to hit the ball consistently straight and solidly time after time. Half the secret to doing that is to develop a swing that you can repeat over and over; the other half is to understand your swing and be able to fix it when something goes wrong.

Through my experience I've come to believe that it's both simpler to understand and easier to repeat an action that's dominated by the big muscles of the legs and upper body instead of the small muscles of the arms and hands. In my swing, the legs and upper body play a dominant role in bringing the club back and through, while the hands and arms stay "quiet," riding the movement of the big muscles.

Most golfers' swings are characterized by excessive hand and wrist motion that requires precise timing to bring the clubface back to the ball squarely at impact. I call it an "arm swing." Some days your timing is pretty good and the results of an arm swing aren't bad. Other days, however, when timing is off, ball-striking doesn't seem nearly as easy.

But if you press the big muscles into a dominant role instead of using mainly arms and hands, you won't have to worry about precise timing anymore—it becomes a matter of bringing the club back and hitting the ball hard. That's why it's a great method for amateurs, who don't get to play that often and thus find it difficult to keep their timing sharp and develop a good "groove." One drawback to this method is that you will give up a little distance, because you can't move the big muscles as fast as you can the smaller ones. But what you lose in yardage, you'll gain in accuracy and consistency.

The swing you're about to learn here is one with which you can be comfortable and feel confident. And the more confident you are in your ability to hit the ball, the better you'll be able to perform in any situation—especially ones involving pressure. I should also add that this swing performs better when the heat is on. Why? Again, because the big muscles are easier to time and control than the smaller ones. Think about it: If you were faced with a shot that you had to pull off and could choose between hitting a full wedge or a half-wedge, which would you pick? Most people would say a full wedge, because the motion employs more of the big muscles of the legs and upper body than a handsy half-shot. That's the idea behind my swing.

I don't mean to give the impression that swinging this way is anything revolutionary. Take a look at Lee Trevino, who's been one of the most accurate drivers and finest players in the game for a lot of years. Note how much body action he incorporates into his swing and how little apparent hand action. Some say Lee's swing is flat and ugly; I think it's beautiful, and his record speaks for itself. Lee's no slouch when it comes to playing with the heat on, either.

Now, to dispel what I consider the four big swing myths.

BIG SWING MYTHS
Myth #1: Keep Your Head Still

Instead: Let Your "Center" Shift Laterally

Odds are that one of the first bits of swing instruction you ever received was to "keep your head still." I know, because I was taught to do the same! The truth is, though, that in order to make a complete weight shift to your right side on the backswing, you have to allow both your head and spine—what I refer to as your "center"— to move laterally to the right. I don't mean a big shift, only about four inches at most. But believe me when I say it's a very important four inches. One of my backswing keys is to move what I call my "left quadrant"—the left shoulder and the area below it—entirely behind the ball when I take the club back to the top. The only way I can do this is by shifting center to the right, which allows me to make a good weight shift, getting about 90 percent of my weight onto my right side. (There are machines that exist that measure your weight distribution at various points in the swing. Try one if you get the chance— the results may surprise you.)

If you don't shift center to the right on the backswing, you can't get your weight fully to the right side, and if that doesn't happen, you won't be able to shift it powerfully to the left on the downswing. Shifting center during the swing is a natural, instinctive motion;

At address, my "center" is balanced in the middle between both feet.

As I swing the club back, however, center shifts to the right along with my weight until it is balanced on my right leg, as indicated by the movement of my head.

At the top I want my weight balanced on my right side and my left shoulder behind the ball.

trying to keep it anchored in one place is unnatural. Young kids do most things naturally, because they haven't learned differently. If you gave a short club to a five-year-old who had never swung one before and told him to hit a ball hard, he wouldn't keep his head down and still. He'd instinctively move all his weight over on his right foot as he brought the club back and his center with it, because it feels powerful. (This goes to show that sometimes we can learn from kids.) Unfortunately, someone's probably going to tell him to keep his head still, and for the rest of his golfing days he'll try his darnedest to keep it from moving while trying to shift his weight and make an aggressive swing at the ball. I don't think you can do one without doing the other. In fact, if I don't allow center to move to the right on my backswing, I end up making a reverse weight shift, which results in a fault called a "dropslide," which I'll describe at the end of this chapter in the "Troubleshooting" section.

Of course, in order to make a complete weight shift from the right side to the left on the downswing, you have to allow center to

This angle affords an excellent view of how my body releases toward the target in the finish: my back and left leg are straight, with center balanced over my left foot.

move to the left as you swing the club down and through, resulting in an increase in consistent, solid contact. In fact, if you keep center completely stationary while you swing, the result is a reverse weight shift; so it's possible if you're an "arm swinger" that you've never actually experienced a true weight shift.

Finally, an additional benefit of shifting center is that it relieves strain on the back at the finish. Over the last several years golfers have been taught to hold their heads down well through impact, so in the finish their bodies are bowed into the shape of a reverse C. Though some players may like the way this position looks, many find they don't like the way it feels after a couple of years because it creates a lot of wear and tear on the lower back. You can see in the pictures of my finish that by letting my upper body release to the target after impact, I'm able to stand perfectly balanced on my left leg, with my body comfortably straight instead of contorted in any manner. With no strain, there's no pain.

. . . and try to keep it there on the backswing. You'll find it's much easier to keep your left arm snug to your chest and keep the handkerchief from falling by letting the left elbow bend slightly.

An excellent drill is to tuck a handkerchief or piece of cloth under your left arm at address . . .

Myth #2: Keep Your Left Arm Straight

Instead: Let It Bend Naturally to Stay Connected

Chances are good that besides being told to keep your head still, you were also told to keep your left arm straight on the backswing. I allow mine to bend, and for a good reason: keeping my left arm ramrod stiff would cause me to become disconnected. It *is* possible to keep your left arm straight and also stay connected, but only if you are flexible enough to make a very big shoulder turn. Cases in point are Sam Snead and Greg Norman. You want to keep your left arm firm, but not consciously stiff. That way, if it wants to bend a little bit when you reach the top, it will.

The key is not to think of swinging your arms back, but to think instead of coiling your body to the right, while simply keeping the left arm riding lightly against the left side of your chest. If you allow the left arm to stretch and lengthen as you reach the top (or "grow"), you'll become disconnected. A good way to practice keeping it there is to put a folded handkerchief under your left arm at address, then swing: the handkerchief should stay where it is until your left arm is pulled away from your body in the follow-through. If it falls to the ground on the backswing, you know you're becoming disconnected. When playing, concentrate on feeling light pressure in your left armpit from takeaway through impact to keep the left arm in the socket.

A hint that you're swinging back correctly is if your backswing feels much shorter. The length of the backswing actually will be shorter; however, your swing arc will be wider, and that's what's most important, because the wider the arc, the more clubhead speed you'll be able to build on the downswing. The reason the arc is wider is because keeping the wrists and forearms quiet on the backswing allows the clubhead to swing back on as low and wide a path as possible.

Myth #3: Left Side Is Dominant, Right Side Is Passive

Instead: Fire Your Right Side!

This idea certainly isn't new: probably the most famous prescription the great player and teacher Tommy Armour ever gave to a student with an ailing game was to "whack the hell out of the ball with your right hand!" Still, there's an awful lot of instruction out there that informs golfers to do the opposite, and to me, that's the wrong way. On the contrary, my favorite downswing key is to start down by shifting my lower body to the left and then to "fire my right side" hard through the ball and toward the target. So long as I start the motion by shifting my weight to my left side and keep my right shoulder from dropping through impact, I can't hit hard enough with my right. That's not to say I'm not pulling with my left side, because I am, but the dominant source of power is from my right side, from the tip of my right toe to the fingertips of my right hand. (A warning here: You have to start the downswing by shifting your weight left, not with the upper body. Otherwise, you'll make the error known as "hitting from the top"—bringing the club down with power generated almost solely by the upper body. A poor swing path and loss of power will result.)

The reason it's all right to use the full force of your right side is because to attain maximum clubhead speed on the downswing, you have to make full use of centrifugal force. To build centrifugal force,

Fire your right side, from the tips of
your fingers to the tips of your toes.

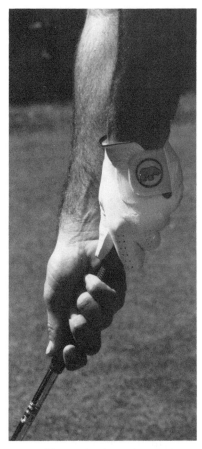

To get the feel of centrifugal force, grip the club with your hands about an inch apart and practice swinging, making an effort to hit hard with your right side.

you need two sides: the inner force, which is the left hand, and the outer force, which is the right hand. If the inner force (left hand) exerts more force than the outer force, then centrifugal force is destroyed and you won't be able to "spring" the shaft. So it's not only okay to hit hard with your right side, it's essential!

An excellent way to feel proper centrifugal force is to hold the club with your hands about an inch apart and make practice swings with your mind on hitting hard with the right side, not pulling with the left.

Myth #4: Keep Your Right Elbow Close to Your Side

Instead: Keep Your Left Elbow Close to Your Side

Classic swing theory preaches the importance of keeping the right elbow tight to the side on the backswing and downswing. I think it's more beneficial to concentrate on keeping the left elbow close to the side and connected on the backswing and downswing. Only by keeping the left elbow close to your side can you fire your right side and be sure of bringing the clubhead down on the correct line and squarely to the ball, which is your protection against swinging the club down on a poor downswing path.

Also, keeping the left elbow close and relatively fixed to the side allows you to maintain centrifugal force on the downswing as you shift center laterally toward the target. If the left elbow comes away from your side as you shift left, you'll lose centrifugal force by blocking the shot.

THE FULL SWING

Those are what I consider the four myths of the golf swing. Now I'd like to take you step by step through my swing, from start to finish. Elapsed time of the average swing is about one-and-a-half seconds, so I obviously don't expect you to think of all this when you hit a ball, nor should you expect to absorb it all in one reading. What you should do is take it slowly and learn the swing part by part, referring back to the text to find out where you should be at a certain point if you aren't sure.

To follow my swing from start to finish, refer to the color section.

1. Address

I described address position in detail in the last chapter, but two things I want to make sure I feel right before I'm ready to start my swing are: 1. the slight tension in my armpits, the insides of my upper arms pressing lightly against my sides; and 2. a light tension on the insides of both thighs.

2. Takeaway

To take the club away, I simply think of keeping my arms firm and shifting the lower point of the triangle with the large muscles of my back and shoulders until the triangle points to my right toe, taking the club with it. I want everything, both the triangle and center, to move away from the ball smoothly and in one piece.

Although it will feel awkward at first, work on keeping the handkerchief snugly under your left arm on the downswing and into the follow-through, letting it drop only when you reach the finish position.

3. Halfway Back

At this point, my head (center) has visibly moved to my right, indicating my weight shift has started and that I'm on my way to getting fully behind the ball. If the weight hasn't started to move at this point, it probably isn't going to move at all. My right elbow has moved in toward my right hip, but the triangle formed by the arms is still intact. The clubface has rotated open so the toe points to the sky. My right leg remains firm, and I'm beginning to feel more tension build in my right thigh. It's crucial that I keep my right leg firm as I bring the club back to prevent center from shifting too far right.

4. At the Top

Your position at the top is one of the most crucial points in the swing, because it is the function of the backswing to put both your body and the club into the best possible position to swing down on the proper downswing path with both power and control, so pay special attention. I like to break it down into four parts: 1. body position; 2. hand/wrist position; 3. clubshaft alignment; and 4. swing plane.

1. Body position: At the top of your backswing, your body should be fully behind the ball. Two of the myths mentioned earlier are clearly violated here: my head has moved, and my left arm is bent (if it were straight, I'd be disconnected). My right leg remains solidly braced—there's a lot of tension in the thigh at this point. My hips and shoulders have turned, but they've remained level with the position they were in at address (if they were tilted, this would signal a reverse pivot), and center has shifted about four inches behind the ball.

2. Hand/wrist position: The clubface can be either square, open, or closed at the top, depending upon how your hands and wrists are positioned. The left hand and wrist are the guide: If the back of the left hand and wrist are cupped, the clubface is open. If the back of the left hand is square with the wrist, the clubface is square; if the wrist is bowed outward, then the face is closed.

The average player is better off with the clubface square at the top (left wrist straight) so that a good, aggressive firing of the right side will result in a full release of the club on the downswing so the face reaches a square position at impact. Stronger players may prefer to play from a slightly open position at the top (left hand slightly cupped). That way, they can release the club very powerfully without worrying about shutting the face too much before impact and hitting

If the back of the left hand forms a straight line with the back of the left wrist and forearm, the clubface is in a square position at the top.

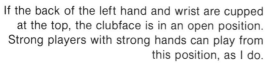

If the back of the left hand and wrist are cupped at the top, the clubface is in an open position. Strong players with strong hands can play from this position, as I do.

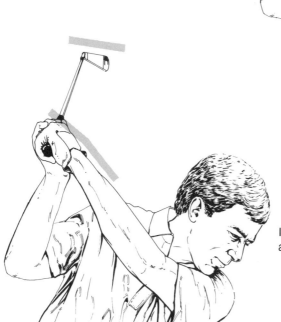

If the back of the left hand and wrist are bowed at the top, the clubface is in a closed position.

Because a shorter shaft forces you to stand closer to the ball, you'll naturally swing on a slightly more upright plane with a wedge (left) than you will with a driver.

a shot that goes left. This is the way I play, allowing me to eliminate the left side of the golf course.

The positions to avoid are closed and very open. If the clubface is closed (left wrist very bowed) at the top, then a strong release of the club on the downswing will only close the face even more, resulting in the shot going left. To hit a reasonably straight shot from a closed position at the top, you have to compensate by blocking your hand release on the downswing, which will cost you power and consistency.

You can play from a very open position at the top (left wrist open), but it requires a very powerful hand release to square the clubface back to the ball by impact—most average players won't be able to, and thus they hit the ball with an open clubface, making the shot go right.

3. Clubshaft alignment: At the top, the clubshaft should be parallel to the line set by the feet, knees, hips, and shoulders. If it points to the right of this line (known as "crossing the line"), you'll swing down on too much of an inside-out path and hit either a hook or push. If it points to the left (known as "laying off"), you'll swing down on an outside-in path and hit either a slice or a pull. Either way, you'll lose consistency. Shaft alignment is impossible to check by yourself, unless you videotape your swing from behind. If you can't do that, have a friend watch, or see a pro. When checking it, use a long-shafted club, such as the driver, and swing into a parallel position at the top.

4. Swing plane: Those words usually scare the casual player, mainly because few understand what they mean. If you think of the path the clubhead takes from the start of the takeaway to the top of the finish as a circle, your swing plane is the angle that the circle is tilted on. Though you can't physically observe this circle, you can observe the position of the left arm, which is the radius of the circle, to get an idea of the angle of your swing plane.

The two extremes of plane are vertical, the way a Ferris wheel turns, and horizontal, the way a merry-go-round turns. Obviously, we can't swing the club on either of those planes but somewhere in between. If you split the two extremes equally, your left arm would be at a 45-degree angle at the top of the backswing. If your arm is below that on a flatter angle, then your plane is on the flat side. If your arm is above the 45-degree mark, your plane is more upright.

Every player has an ideal swing plane, equal to a line drawn straight from the ball through the middle of your neck. However, plane will vary from player to player because the distance you stand from the ball depends on height and posture. A taller player will naturally swing on a more upright plane than someone shorter, because the taller player stands closer to the ball. You'll automatically swing on the proper plane as long as you remain connected. Letting the left arm come away from the chest on the backswing can cause your plane to become too upright or too flat. Understand that your own swing plane will vary slightly from club to club, because shaft length forces you to stand slightly different distances from the ball. Thus you'll swing a wedge on a more upright plane than you will a driver, but only slightly.

5. Starting Down

The first move down is to shift the weight toward the left side, keeping the right hip level (I like to get the feeling that I'm kicking from inside my right leg), then fire the right side of the upper body. My left side is leading because my hips are moving first toward the target, while my right side is rocketing from the ground up.

6. Halfway Down

At this point I'm hitting full force with my right side (the outer force), using my big muscles. My left arm (the inner force) is staying close to my chest and my hips remain level—the right side hasn't dropped—as I bend the shaft on the downswing.

7. Impact

At impact, my hips are still level and driving to the left, about 85 percent of my weight is on my left side, and center has returned to the position it was in at address—though my head has not moved past the ball. My arms have returned to the triangular position they were in at address—the right has straightened and is releasing the club fully so that the clubface is solidly on the ball at this split second.

8. Post-Impact

At this point in my swing, a split second after impact, I want to feel as though my right arm is extending fully outward and touching the target. My right arm has indeed fully straightened, driving the clubhead straight down the target line. My hips are still level, weight is mostly on my left side, and center has shifted about four inches in front where the ball was positioned, caused by releasing the back.

9. Finish

A controlled ending: My entire body has released so my spine is straight and free of strain. My center of gravity is balanced comfortably on the ball of my left foot and the hips remain level. My left arm has finally come away from my chest, a result of the force of the swing. Although I finish with my body upright, the hands and club are still on plane and my chest points to the target.

RHYTHM AND TEMPO

You've probably noticed differences in rhythm and tempo among your usual playing partners. One person might swing with a graceful motion, the clubhead building speed through impact the way a string of cars on a roller coaster builds speed through the bottom of a large dip. Meanwhile, another guy may look as if he's trying to beat out a fire with a shovel. Rhythm is the smoothness, or evenness, of the overall motion; any jerkiness or abruptness is nonrhythmic. Tempo is the amount of time it takes from start to finish of the swing.

Rhythm and tempo usually depend on your personality type. If you're the energetic, quick-moving type, it will probably be reflected in a faster swing. Ben Hogan swung fast; so do Arnold Palmer and Lanny Wadkins. If you're of a calmer demeanor, you'll probably swing at a slower, easier pace, like Jay Haas, Larry Mize, or Payne Stewart.

If you're an "arm swinger," rhythm and tempo are very important, because your sense of timing depends on them. With the connected swing, timing will come easier, since keying on the large muscles will naturally result in an even, rhythmic motion, and keeping the left arm connected and releasing the club on the downswing will get the clubface back to square at impact. If you are jerking the clubhead away from the ball at the start of the takeaway (and you'll never see a good player do this), it's a sign that you're using the small muscles of your hands and arms too much, and you should quiet them down.

> **Rhythm is the smoothness, or evenness of the overall motion. Tempo is the amount of time it takes from start to finish of the swing.**

TROUBLESHOOTING

As you've probably found out by now, there's a lot more to hitting the ball than learning how to swing the club correctly. Although I believe the connection method breaks it down into its simplest, most natural form, the swing is still a pretty complex mechanism, given to minor breakdowns (and occasional major ones) that result in ball-striking problems.

Connection: The insides of both my left and right upper arms remain snug to my sides as the club moves back, keeping the arms "in the sockets."

Disconnection: My right upper arm and elbow have moved away from my body, causing the clubhead to swing back on an overly outside path.

You certainly don't need anyone to tell you when something's gone wrong because your shot will be a clear indication, whether it's some form of a slice, hook, top, fat, or shank. After finishing this section, you'll be able to identify what you did wrong according to the type of shot that resulted. First, though, I'll define what I feel are the four main pitfalls that can occur: disconnection, the "dropslide," reverse pivoting, and "holding on."

Disconnection: My left upper arm and elbow have come out of the socket and disconnected; the clubhead moves back on an overly inside path.

Connection: My left arm stays connected with the inside of the upper arm snug to my chest, resulting in proper swing plane.

Disconnection

If the left arm separates from the left side on the backswing or on the downswing before impact, you're disconnected. Players often try to swing their hands too high on the backswing, resulting in disconnection and a swing plane that's too upright. Less common is becoming disconnected by dropping the left arm too low, so the swing is too flat. Both of these forms of disconnection will cause poor clubhead path on the backswing, leading to poor clubhead path on the downswing.

Bear in mind, though, that you can make a connected backswing

Disconnection: My left arm has come away from my chest, resulting in poor swing plane (too upright) and poor club alignment at the top.

Connection: The insides of both upper arms are still snug to the sides of my chest through impact. Note that the toe of the club has passed the heel, indicating a good release.

and still become disconnected on the downswing. The cause stems from hitting with the small muscles of the hands and forearms without hitting enough with the big muscles of the legs, back, and shoulders. Then the left arm comes away from the body and downswing path suffers. Remember, its okay to hit hard with your hands, but only if you also hit hard with your body, which will keep the left arm connected with the chest. Directional problems such as slicing and hooking result from disconnection.

My own swing was disconnected when I played in college, as you can see by checking the sequences in Evolution of a Golfer on the following pages.

Disconnection: My left arm has come away from my side through impact. The toe of the club has barely passed the heel at this late stage, indicating that it was most likely still open at impact, causing the ball to go right.

Disconnection: My right arm has become disconnected and moved away from my side. The toe of the clubhead has rotated around past the heel, so the face was probably closed at impact, causing this shot to go left.

EVOLUTION OF A GOLFER

Age nine: I'm putting to work on the practice tee the fundamentals that my father taught me.

In the following swing sequence photos, note the differences between my college-age swing and how I swing the club today.

A Stance looks stable and the grip looks fine, but the arms are much too tense, causing the upper arms to disconnect from the sides of the chest.

B A pretty good, low, one-piece takeaway, though, again, the arms are way too stiff.

C Right here you can clearly see that my right elbow has come disconnected from my side.

D I'm not flexible enough to keep my left arm straight without becoming disconnected at the top.

E Despite the earlier disconnection, here's a pretty good example of leg drive.

F Because I became disconnected, whether the clubface was sufficiently square at impact to produce a reasonably straight shot depended on whether my timing was exactly right.

G Although my lower body is turning and moving toward the target, I'm working hard to keep my head down and still, putting strain on my back . . .

H . . . and resulting in what's known as a reverse "C" at the finish, which eventually leads to back injuries for most players who swing into this position.

A   **B**   **C**

D   E   F

G   H

The Dropslide

A "dropslide" is a downswing error characterized by letting the right shoulder drop downward and the left hip slide toward the target at the start of the downswing as the weight is transferred to the left side, instead of keeping the shoulders and hips level. The result is that the lower body slides laterally toward the target, instead of turning powerfully. The body slides out too far left and the hands don't get a chance to catch up and square the ball at impact, so at its worst, a dropslide causes high, weak, faded drives and fat (hitting behind the ball) iron shots. But dropsliding can occur in lesser degrees, with less-devastating effects on the shot. I still dropslide slightly once in a while, and when I do I know it immediately, because the resulting shot is either pulled or mishit toward the toe or heel.

Reverse Pivot

The worst form of the reverse pivot occurs when the proper weight shift is reversed, with the weight moving to the left side on the backswing, then falling back to the right side on the downswing. Reverse pivoting is an easy pitfall to fall into because it can be very subtle—often you won't realize you're doing it. Signs that it's happening are a loss of distance (since lack of forward weight shift on the downswing will cost you clubhead speed) and a loss of accuracy.

Again, the good player is not immune to reverse pivoting: I check at least once a week to make sure I'm shifting my weight properly, and I recommend that you do the same. If I'm not getting my left quadrant fully behind the ball on the backswing, I know I'm not getting all of my weight on my right side. At the finish, all of my weight should be on my left foot, allowing me to step toward the target easily with my right foot. If you aren't able to take a step easily, you aren't getting your weight on to your left side properly on the downswing.

Holding On

In order to square the clubface to the ball at impact, you have to release the club with the hands, letting the right hand rotate over the left through the bottom of the swing arc. Failing to release the club, a fault that I call "holding on," will result in an open face at impact and a shot that goes to the right.

Many amateurs hold on through impact because they mistrust the release, since it feels to them as if they are shutting the face completely before contact. I once had a pro-am partner whose overall swing mechanics were darned good, except he froze his wrists terribly on the downswing. Because of this, his clubface was always open at impact, so he sliced everything. After a few holes of watching him do this we had to wait a few minutes for the group ahead of us, so I took him aside on the tee and told him what his problem was. "Do me a favor," I said, "try to hit this next tee shot with the toe of your driver."

"I couldn't," he responded. "I'll snap-hook it dead left."

I asked if he had ever actually snap-hooked a shot.

"No, never," he said, "but I will if I do what you tell me. I'll hit the ball with the toe of the club."

"You won't actually hit it with the toe," I told him. "It's going to feel like you will, but you'll actually be squaring the clubface to the ball." I demonstrated the split-hand grip and got him to take a few practice swings with it. "How does that feel?" I asked.

"Awful—like I'm closing the face completely before it reaches the bottom of the swing."

"That's good," I said. "That's how it should feel. I want you to have that same feeling when you hit this drive."

"No way!" he pleaded. "I'll smother it dead left!"

"Haven't you ever had to hook a shot around a tree and really tried to shut the face quick, only to have the ball fly straight as a string?"

"Yes, I guess I have. . . ." he answered.

He took a few more practice swings with his hands apart, then stepped up and rifled one high and down the middle, with just a hint of left-to-right fade at the end.

"Incredible!" he murmured in disbelief, while watching the ball drop in the fairway about 250 yards out. "It felt like I was shutting the clubface completely."

"When, in fact," I added, "it was still slightly open at impact, since the ball faded a little."

The moral of this story is feels can fool you. Don't let what you feel fool you into holding onto the club through impact. Hit hard with your right side and let your hands release—though it may feel at first as if you're shutting the face too soon, you actually aren't.

> "Feels" can fool you. Don't let what you feel fool you into holding onto the club through impact.

Starting Down with the Upper Body

I already said that my main downswing goals are to start down by shifting my lower body to the left, then fire my right side. If you get this sequence out of sync and start with the downswing with the

A good drill for learning to initiate the downswing by shifting your weight to the left side is to put a golf ball under the outside of your right foot and use it to push off of when starting down.

upper body, you'll leave your weight on your right side and force the clubhead into an outside-in swing path. The resulting shot will start left of the target line and either continue straight or curve left or right, depending upon what clubface alignment was at impact.

A PAIR OF ACES

To close the swing chapter, I decided to present sequences of what are considered to be two of the prettiest, most efficient, most mechanically perfect golf swings you'll ever find: Sam Snead and Greg Norman.

First, the basics. Both Sam and Greg's grips are excellent; neither too weak nor too strong. Both players' feet are spread shoulder-width, providing a solid foundation to swing on, and their posture is fine. Note how the insides of their upper arms are in contact with, or "connected to" their sides. Notice also the triangle formed by the arms and shoulders.

The takeaway: That first 18 inches the clubhead travels away from the ball is one of the most crucial parts of the swing. There's no breakdown of the wrists or in the triangle by either player as the club is taken away. That's because the work is being done with the big muscles in a unified, "one-piece" motion. Using the big muscles in the takeaway also makes for a slow, steady start.

At this point, it's plain that both players' weight has moved to their right sides and that their left shoulders are already behind the ball. A notable difference, though, is that Greg's arms are extended farther from his body than Sam's—typical of a power hitter.

At the top, both players have turned their backs fully to the target. Their hips have turned a great deal, but only as a result of their tremendous shoulder turn. Neither one has "overswung," since both clubshafts are parallel to the ground and have not dipped below that point. Note the difference in balance: Sam's weight is loaded perfectly on the inside of his right foot, while Greg's has moved slightly onto the outside of his right foot.

Both of these players really excel at the start of the downswing. The first move down is a push off the right foot as the lower body shifts toward the target and the weight moves to the left side. The upper body follows in a smooth, unhurried manner.

Here, in both cases, most of the weight is on the left side while the right side remains level and firing hard; meanwhile the head stays behind the ball.

At impact, both players' arms have returned to the triangular shape they were in at address. Also, despite the force each one is putting into the downswing, they're maintaining excellent balance and control, and that their left arms remain close to, or "connected," to their left sides. One way that Greg differs from Sam at this point is that Greg's hips have slid further toward the target, bringing his weight more onto the outside of his left foot.

Both players have fully released the club—the toe pointing to the sky and the right arm extended down the target line—while the head remains behind where the ball was positioned. One difference is that although Sam has risen up on his right toe, his foot stays still, whereas Greg's right leg is dragging slightly toward the target—another trait typical of the big hitter.

At the finish, Sam looks perfect: His weight is almost completely balanced on his left foot and his back has released toward the target so he's standing straight and without strain. Greg's weight is also balanced on his left side, although his back hasn't released completely, but instead has stayed behind, causing his body to form a slight reverse "C" position.

4
THROUGH THE BAG:
USING THE DIFFERENT CLUBS

Although the swing stays virtually the same with every club, setup and ball position should vary among woods, long irons, middle irons, and short irons. With driver and fairway woods, I spread my feet wide, just outside shoulder width, and play the ball opposite my left heel. With long irons, stance narrows so the outside halves are outside shoulder width and the ball is about one ball width behind the left heel. For middle irons, bring the feet a little closer together—to about shoulder width—and play the ball about one ball width ahead of center. Finally, with short irons, feet should be just inside shoulder width, your stance slightly open, and the ball opposite center.

Some players advocate playing the ball in the same place—off the

The thrill of victory: I make a happy shake of the fist after sinking a birdie putt on the third hole of a sudden-death play-off to defeat Calvin Peete in the 1986 Houston Open.

UTILITY WOODS VS. LONG IRONS

The clubs that most amateurs seem to have trouble hitting are the long irons. These straight-faced clubs require both hand strength and clubhead speed in order to be hit well, and if you don't catch the ball solidly, you usually get a much-less-than-satisfactory result. Anyone who has trouble hitting his or her 2- and 3-irons should seriously consider replacing them with a 5- or 6-wood. These clubs have more mass and longer shafts than long irons, allowing you to build more clubhead speed through impact. Their larger, bulkier heads instill more confidence in making solid contact and glide smoothly through moderate rough in which a long-iron would tangle.

If, on the other hand, you're a long, straight hitter, you may want to consider putting a 1-iron in your bag. The 1-iron is a club that only a rare few can hit well, since it requires a great deal of clubhead speed and excellent clubface alignment at impact to get the shot off the ground and keep it straight. Even if you have little success with the 1-iron off the fairway, you may be able to hit it off a tee. If so, it is still valuable to you on holes with tight driving areas.

left heel—with every club, but I like my way because although keeping the ball forward with woods puts it in the best possible position to sweep away solidly with the shallow downswing path of these long-shafted clubs, progressively shifting ball position back as the shaft gets shorter helps you to make an increasingly descending blow, which produces a high trajectory with the shorter irons. To me, the longer you carry the ball, the better. In the old days, it was an

driver

3-wood

advantage distancewise to hit low, driving shots that would bounce and roll a long way after landing. But today's courses are so well watered and soft, due to advancements in irrigation and sprinkler systems, that most shots, even low-driving ones, stop quickly when they hit the ground. So these days it's to the advantage of every player, even shorter hitters, to carry the ball as far as possible.

2-iron

5-iron

7-iron

9-iron

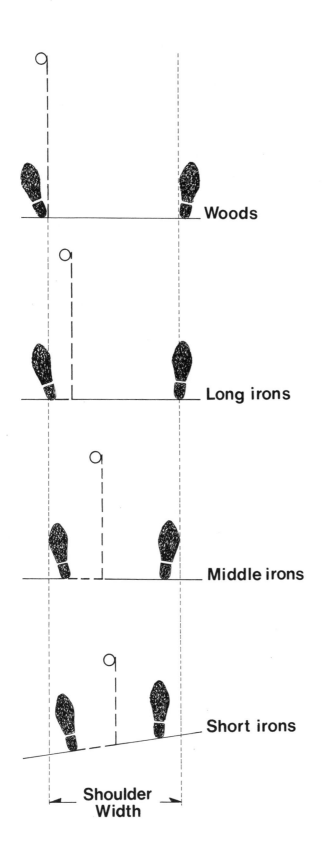

Woods

Long irons

Middle irons

Short irons

Shoulder Width

Play the ball off your left heel with the driver and fairway woods, one ball width behind that for long irons, two ball widths back for middle irons, and in the center of the stance for short irons.

BACKSPIN

On top of all the reasons that were just mentioned in favor of varying ball position according to club, there's one more: playing it farther back increases the chances of hitting the ball first, which increases the amount of backspin you'll get.

If I were posed the following choices . . .

Most amateurs are:
A. Enamored of backspin
B. Delighted with backspin
C. Mystified by backspin
D. Want more backspin
E. All of the above

. . . my answer would be E. The shot that hits the green, bounces once, then spins backward, is the one that my pro-am partners envy the most, hands down.

First of all, you should know that every well-struck shot has backspin on it—it has to in order to rise in the air and hold its line. To prove it, take a striped range ball and address it so the stripe is perpendicular to your target line; then hit a short pitch. You should be able to see by the revolution of the stripe that the ball is spinning backward. So if your shots aren't stopping very quickly, it isn't because they don't have any backspin; it's just that they aren't

BALATA VS. SURLYN

These days, golf balls are made with one of two different types of covers: balata or surlyn. Balata was originally a natural rubber derived from a tree, but most manufacturers produce it synthetically now. The balata cover is thinner and softer, providing greater feel and more spin. The disadvantage of balata is that the cover is somewhat fragile—mishit the ball by blading it and the leading edge of the club is liable to cut clear through, producing what's known as a "smile." This is the chief reason most higher handicappers shy away from balata-covered balls.

Surlyn, on the other hand, is a man-made substance that was developed as an alternative to the less durable balata. A surlyn cover is thicker and harder than balata, making it much tougher to cut, but also making it feel harder at impact and allowing less spin.

What's inside the cover also varies. If it's a wound ball (rubber windings surrounding a small, rubber or liquid core), the ball will have more "give" to it and thus will feel softer at impact.

A solid ball, in contrast, has a one-piece center made of hard rubber within the cover (it's also called a "two-piece" ball). This type of ball will give you more distance but has a harder feel at impact and is more difficult to spin because it has less give.

Although certain types of balls will give you certain advantages for playing one shot to another, there is a rule on tour that you must use the same type of ball from the start to the finish of a round—no switching to a ball with different characteristics midround.

spinning very fast, so whatever spin exists is killed on the first bounce so the ball releases and rolls. How much spin you're able to put on the ball depends on certain factors.

Lie

It should be clean, with the grain of the grass growing toward the target. Anything getting in between the clubface and the ball—tall blades of grass, for instance—decreases the amount of spin you'll get. If the grain is growing toward you, the leading edge of the clubface will scrape some of the grass up as it approaches the ball and trap it in between at impact, reducing spin.

Wind

If it's in your face, it will throw the ball up higher, causing it to land on a sharper angle and thus stop quicker. Thus, any backspin on the ball will be more effective at making it back up. A tailwind, on the other hand, will push the ball so it lands on a shallower angle, skips forward upon landing, and is less likely to back up.

Club Selection

The steeper the angle on which the clubhead approaches the ball, the more backspin it yields, so you'll get the most spin from the short irons and progressively less as you move up through the middle irons, long irons, fairway woods, and driver.

Clubhead Speed

It's no mystery why guys like Greg Norman and Mark McCumber can really make the ball dance—it's because they swing down harder than most people and thus get more spin. Because more clubhead speed results in more backspin, you'll often see players laying up between 110 and 90 yards from the green of a par five with their second shot, even though they could get it closer. The reason is so they can hit a full wedge shot, putting more spin on the ball so it will stop faster.

Those are factors that influence the amount of spin that can be put on the ball and whether it will stop quickly or even back up. The more factors in your favor, the better the chances the ball will bite. But all of this still doesn't guarantee that the ball will back up when it hits the green—whether it sucks back or not also depends on the characteristics of the putting surface.

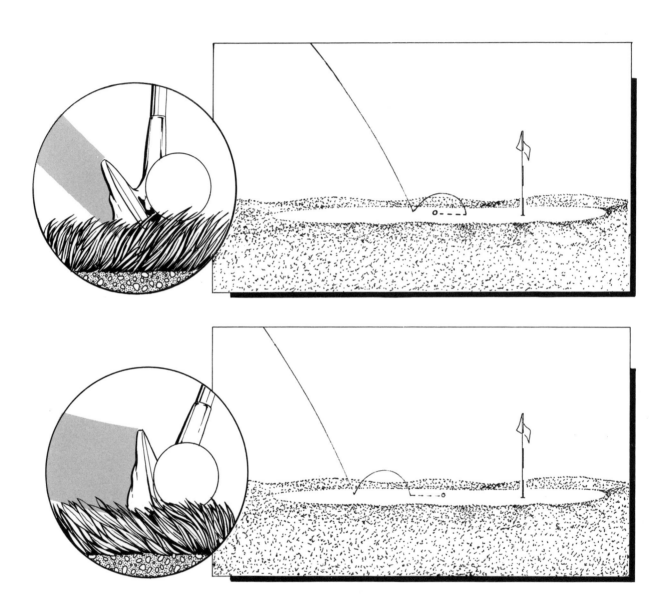

Many amateurs fail to realize that if the grass is growing toward them (away from the target), they won't be able to get maximum bite on the shot, even if all other conditions favor backspin.

Speed and Firmness of Surface

No matter how much backspin you put on a shot, you'll never be able to back it up on a gym floor. Nor can you back it up if the surface of the green is very hard and fast. Take note of how many shots you see back up next time you watch the Masters or U.S. Open; both tournaments are notorious for the firmness and slickness of the surfaces. In contrast, if rain has softened up the surfaces of the greens, the players will have a great deal of control over how the ball reacts on the greens.

There. *All* the factors that determine the degree of backspin that can be put on a shot and whether the ball will back up when it lands. When you really see one scoot back fast, it's usually because all or most of these factors were favorable. Bear in mind also that backspin doesn't always work positively for you—any player who has ever landed a shot on a green only to have it suck back and roll off the front will attest to that.

MY CLUBS
Here's what I keep in my bag.

Woods
- Driver: MacGregor Muirfield Metal Wood, 7 degrees, 43½″
- 3-wood: Metal Wood Brassie, 11 degrees
- 4-wood: Metal Wood Cleek, 16 degrees

Irons
- 2—PW: Muirfield VIP
- SW: Cleveland Classic

Putters
- Ping Zing 2
- Acushnet Bull's-eye with flange

Notes
- X100 shaft flex on woods; S400 on irons. (Of all club specifications, having the right shaft flex is most important. See your pro to make sure that the shaft flex of your clubs is correct for you.)
- Swing weight ranges between D2½ and D3.
- Grips built up ¹⁄₃₂″ oversize.
- All clubs standard lie; all irons standard loft.
- I generally use the Ping to putt with but occasionally switch over to the Bull's-eye, which has a much different look and feel.
- If playing conditions are windy and hard, I may take the 4-wood out of the bag to make room for a 1-iron (Muirfield VIP).

5
SHOTMAKING: CURVE BALLS
AND OTHER SHOTS

To throw a curve ball, a baseball pitcher intentionally puts sidespin on the ball when he releases it. The faster he can make it spin, the sharper the pitch will curve. Golfers can also intentionally apply spin to their shots to make the ball move in a particular direction. (The problem of most amateurs is that they unintentionally put *too* much sidespin on their shots, causing a hook or slice.)

You should always plan to put some kind of spin on the ball, mainly because it's too difficult to hit the ball perfectly straight time after time. The clubhead must be moving on a precise inside-to-square-to-inside-downswing path, and the clubface must be precisely square at the point of impact. Meanwhile, the clubhead is moving somewhere between 80 and 100 miles per hour through the bottom of the swing. The fact is, it takes a certain amount of luck to hit a shot perfectly straight. The only player I ever heard of who actually tried to play a straight ball was Byron Nelson, and all I can figure is that Byron had a talent that very few possess. Most players are better off planning for a little sidespin and aiming slightly away from the target to allow for the ball to curve back to it.

The direction and trajectory of a shot are caused by the downswing path the clubhead moves on and the alignment of the clubface at impact. In a perfect swing, the clubhead is swung back on a slightly inside path, with the clubface gradually rotating clockwise as it moves away from the ball so that the toe points straight up when the shaft reaches the nine o'clock position. On the downswing, the clubhead returns to the ball on the same path, with the toe gradually rotating counterclockwise on the downswing so the clubface is closing through impact. This combination of clubhead path and clubface alignment at impact will start the ball straight down the target line and impart a slight amount of counterclockwise spin on the ball, making it draw just a little.

Putting different types of sidespin—either clockwise or counter-

No matter in which direction I want to bend the shot, I always align the clubface directly at the target.

clockwise—and varying amounts of sidespin on your shots becomes a matter of aligning the clubface and the lines of your body (feet, knees, hips, and shoulders) in the proper directions at address to set up the proper swing path and clubface alignment at impact, which will result in the direction and amount of spin desired.

IDENTIFYING YOUR NATURAL SHOT

Your "natural shot" is the direction the ball moves when you aren't trying to aim it in any particular direction. As mentioned previously, hitting a shot perfectly straight is pretty tough and more a matter of luck than skill in most cases. Practically everyone, if he or she sets the clubface square to the target, then aligns his or her body square to the target line and hits the ball, will apply a certain amount of sidespin in one direction or the other due to his or her individual combination of rhythm, body motion, and hand action. My natural shot is from right to left, as is Tom Watson's, Greg Norman's, and Fred Couples's. Players whose natural shot is a fade include Jack Nicklaus, Lee Trevino, Craig Stadler, and Bruce Lietzke. Remember, I don't mean a lot of movement here, just a very slight curve.

Your natural shot is the direction in which the ball *usually* moves, but it may not always curve that way. You may normally hit a fade from a square stance, but there may be days when you set up square and get a draw. That's why it's a good idea to hit some practice shots before each round—not only to warm up, but also to find out what kind of day it is: right to left or left to right.

Fades and Slices

To hit a fade, which moves slightly from left to right, I aim the clubface squarely at the target, but instead of aligning my body parallel to the target, I set up a little open—aiming my feet, knees, hips, and shoulders slightly left of the target line. What this does is open the clubface slightly in relation to the swing path, resulting in a small degree of slice-spin that will make the ball shift a few yards to the right at the peak of its flight. The more I want to curve the ball, to hit an intentional slice, the more I open my stance.

Draws and Hooks

To hit a right-to-left draw, do the opposite: Aim the clubface down the target line, then close your body alignment by aiming slightly right of the target. For a hook, aim your body even farther left and make sure you release the club at impact.

THE KEY TO HITTING CURVES

If you've followed the previous instructions but aren't getting the results you want, make sure that you're swinging the club normally along the lines on which you've set your body. A tip that always seems to help is actually to pick out a secondary target to align your body with; then concentrate on swinging your hands straight out toward it in the follow-through.

To hit a left-to-right shot, I open my stance (above) by aiming the lines of my body—feet, knees, hips, shoulders—left of target, as opposed to a square alignment (top right). The farther the stance is opened, the more the shot will curve. To bend the ball from right to left, close the stance (bottom right), aiming the body lines to the right of the target. The more closed the stance, the more the shot will curve.

The strategy behind bending the ball: If I aim away from my target and try to curve the ball back to it, three things can happen—it curves as much as I'd planned, a little more, or a little less. No matter what, it ends up on the short grass.

THE STRATEGY OF BENDING THE BALL

It's not only easier to hit a shot that bends, as opposed to going dead straight, but it also increases the percentages of putting the ball near the target and keeping it out of trouble. Imagine a par four where the optimum landing area off the tee is the center of the fairway. If you try to hit the ball straight to that point but push or pull it, you miss the fairway to the right or left. If, however, you elect to aim down the right side of the fairway and play a draw, odds increase that the ball

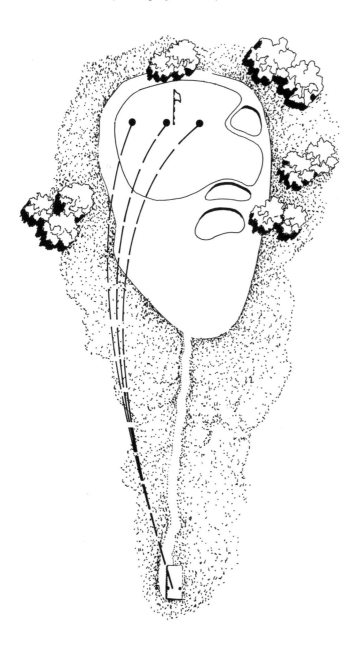

The same idea applied to an approach shot.

will find the short grass. If it draws as planned, you're in the center. If it draws a little less than planned, you're on the right side; if it draws a little more than planned, you're on the left side. Whichever occurs, the ball stays out of the rough. This same principle applies to hitting greens.

The reason for learning to bend the ball both ways is so that you can aim away from trouble and bring the shot back toward the target, decreasing the chances of hitting into a hazard. This is playing the percentages, something that I'll talk more about in Chapter 12, on course control.

HIGH BALLS AND LOW BALLS

Intentional hooks and slices are great for bending the ball around any trees that get in your way, but sometimes you'll be better off going over the tree or hitting under the limbs.

High Balls

The best way to get more height is simply to take a higher-lofted club. But if you need height and distance, you can increase the angle of the clubface slightly by playing the ball about one ball width farther forward than usual but keeping your hands behind the ball. Swing normally and the ball will fly higher and slightly shorter. Remember to stay down and through with this shot—mishit it and the ball will end up rattling around in the tree branches.

Swing normally . . . remember to stay down.

Low Balls

Keeping the ball low will not only help you get out of the woods, but will also help maintain control on approach shots into strong wind. The lower you hit the shot, the less the wind will affect it, and the more control you'll have. Again, the easiest way to keep a shot low is to use a club with lower loft. To reduce the loft by about one-half of a club, play the ball about one ball width behind center. To bend the shot to the right, keep the clubface open through impact by maintaining a firm left hand and wrist on the downswing to keep the right hand from rolling over the left. To bend it left, let the right hand roll over freely through impact.

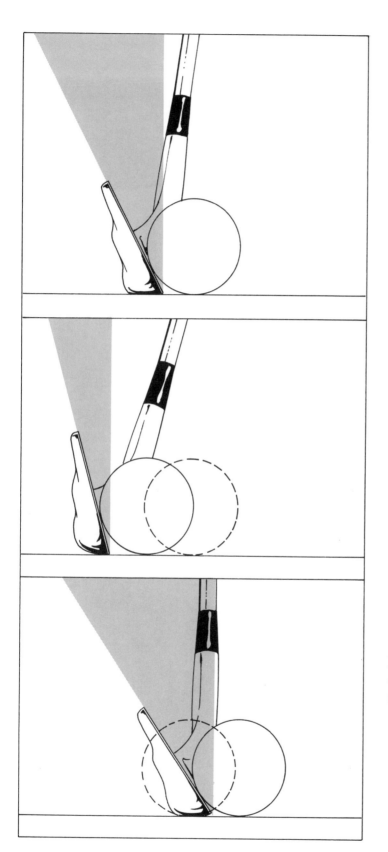

If your ball position is normal at address, you'll make full use of the club's loft (top). By playing the ball back in your stance (center), you effectively decrease the loft of the clubface. Likewise, playing the ball farther forward (bottom) adds loft.

To get a little more height on a particular club, play the ball slightly more forward (right) than usual (left).

To hit the shot lower than usual, play the ball farther
back in your stance than normal.

6
PUTTING: THE BOTTOM LINE IS THE BOTTOM OF THE CUP

Putting, to me, takes more guts than any other part of the game because it's mostly mental, requiring little physical ability—the answers to why you are or aren't having success on the greens will be found mainly between your ears. Putting also takes guts because it's the end of the line—the finish of the hole—and often ends up making or breaking your score there. What I mean is, most of the pressure of what you score on a particular hole comes down to putting. For example, suppose you pull your tee shot on a par four into the rough. You know that there's still the distinct possibility of making up for that shot and saving par by hitting a good recovery to the green or by getting your second shot near enough to the green to chip close and tap in for par. But things don't always work out that way (and you should know from experience that they often don't), and instead you might be left with a 10-footer for your four. Then it comes down to you, your putter, and your ability to use it to roll the ball across that 10 feet of green and into the cup. There's no recovery shot to save a missed par putt, or any putt for that matter—although you can make amends for a bad tee shot or stray approach, a missed putt is a stroke that's gone forever.

When you come right down to it, you're only as good at chipping, pitching, and green-side sand play as you are at putting, because what good is it to get the ball consistently within five feet or so if you can't consistently hole the putts? What good is it to hit an approach shot tight if you can't knock it in for birdie? Worse than that is the blow to the psyche suffered when, after rifling a 3-iron to five feet, the putt slides by the lip. Or the frustration of facing a 20-footer for birdie one minute, then backhanding your third putt for bogey the next. I think you'll agree that you'll never become a complete golfer or fulfill your true scoring potential until you become a good putter.

There's another reason why putting takes a lot of guts for tour players, who regularly play on surfaces that are lightning fast. Many

> **You'll never become a complete golfer or fulfill your true scoring potential until you become a good putter.**

Second round of the '89 U.S. Open. My 63rd stroke—a birdie putt—on 18 looked good, but just slid by. I tapped in for 64, tying the course record, held by Ben Hogan.

times we'll face a short downhill putt that could leave a comebacker twice that length should the first miss the hole. With that consequence in mind, you'd better have a certain amount of intestinal fortitude when you step up to that downhiller or you're not going to survive out there. And when your putter goes cold, it can have a negative effect on the rest of your game: You find yourself trying to force your approach shots close to the hole because you haven't made anything all day. The need to hit good approach shots puts pressure on your driving, and soon everything is out of whack. That's why most pros would rather avoid a slump with the putter than with any other club in the bag.

Despite the many aspects involved in putting that are all too easy to get wrapped up in, from stroke mechanics to green reading, when all is said and done and you're standing over the ball, don't ever lose sight of the fact that all you can do then is aim the ball and hit it.

GREAT PUTTERS ARE BORN, BUT GOOD PUTTERS CAN BE MADE

It's my opinion that the really great putters—guys like Billy Casper, Bob Charles, Ben Crenshaw, Tom Watson—are born, not made. Certain people simply possess a feel for the greens that can't be taught. They naturally seem to have solid mechanics and feel, as well as good instincts for reading greens. I've noticed, too, that the best putters I've ever played with also exude an extremely positive attitude and believe in themselves on the greens—it's as if they know they're going to sink the putt instead of hoping to.

Although I don't think greatness can be learned, I do believe that a person who is only a mediocre putter can become a good putter with a little effort.

The trick to being a good putter is to recognize that there are two aspects to putting, and you have to be good at both. The first is the stroke: you must be able to make a solid, repeating stroke that rolls the ball in the direction you want it to go at the approximate speed you desire (it sounds simple, but it's not). Besides being mechanically sound, your stroke should also allow for "feel"—sensitivity to the clubhead (where it is and how fast it's traveling) and the speed of the greens.

WHAT'S A STIMP METER?

You may hear that the greens for a certain tournament ranked a certain number on the "stimp meter," say 9.2 or 10.7. What does that mean? First, a stimp meter is a narrow steel chute, three feet long, that's used to gauge the speed and consistency of putting greens. It was invented in 1949 by Ed Stimpson, the 1935 Massachusetts amateur champion. To measure a green's "stimp," or speed, a flat part of the surface is first chosen. One end of the stimp meter is rested on the green. Then the other end is raised until the chute is at a 20-degree angle. A ball is placed six inches from the higher end and allowed to roll down and onto the surface. Usually, three balls are rolled, with the highest and lowest disqualified and the middle, or "mean," number measured. Then, three balls are rolled in the opposite direction, with the mean again measured. The two mean numbers are added and divided by two, and you have the stimp reading for that green (for example, a stimp of 9.2 means the average number of feet the ball rolled was nine feet, two inches). The greens on an average PGA Tour course measure between 9 and 9.6, while they will usually be faster, somewhere between 10 and 12, on a U.S. Open course.

The second aspect is green reading—the ability to take into account all existing outside conditions that could affect the particular putt in question and synthesize that information into a prediction of the line the ball will take to the cup and at what speed you have to hit it to get it to take that line.

It won't help to be good in one category and not the other. You may be an excellent green reader, but if you can't stroke the ball along the line you want, it's no good. And I don't care if you've got the best stroke in the world; you'll be sunk if you haven't got a decent clue as to how the ball will react to the speed, contour, and grain of the green. To be successful on tour, you have to be able to adapt to different conditions on the greens every week, sometimes from day to day. The fastest surfaces we face all year are at Augusta and the U.S. Open, and you can bet that on the last day of both those tournaments the greens are just as fast as the greenskeeper can make them.

BUILDING A SOLID STROKE

It's been said by a lot of players that putting is a completely different game from that played from tee to green, and, in fact, they do differ a great deal. When you hit the ball with a full swing, strength is definitely more at a premium than finesse: the point of the swing is to build maximum, controlled clubhead speed while using differently angled club faces to regulate the distance the ball goes. Tee-to-green shots are played through the air over hazards or occasionally bumped along the ground.

Conversely, when putting, you have to roll the ball, negotiating head-on hazards that exist in the green's surface, such as dips, mounds, and tiers. The same putter is used for all lengths of putts, with distance controlled by how hard you swing the clubhead, which directly depends on your sense of feel and finesse.

There is one thing, however, which the full swing and putting have exactly in common: the object of both actions is to return the clubface squarely to the ball in order to start it moving down the intended line. Although I have specific beliefs on how everyone should go about doing so with a 5-iron or driver (as you found out in Chapter 3), I don't when it concerns the putting stroke. I don't think anyone can say that there's a specific right or wrong way to stroke a putt. The evidence is in the variety of styles displayed by history's great putters. Billy Casper uses a lot of wrist action, Bob Charles is all arms and shoulders, and Ben Crenshaw and Jack Nicklaus's strokes are combinations of all three of these elements. There's no way you can say that one of these methods is better or worse than another,

---

Six Fundamentals of Putting:
1. **Grip**
2. **Balance**
3. **Steadiness of center . . .**

because all four of these players are great at getting the ball in the hole. And that's really the only true yardstick for measuring whether a stroke is right or wrong, good or bad. If the stroke succeeds in sinking a lot of putts and avoiding three-putts, then it's right, no matter what it looks like. Take Isao Aoki. As unorthodox as he is, who's going to tell him he's doing it wrong, in view of the number of putts he makes.

There are a few common links, though, that all masters of the flatstick share and that I think of as the "six fundamentals" of putting. They are as follows: 1. grip; 2. balance; 3. steadiness of center; 4. eyes directly over the line, but not ahead of the ball; 5. square shoulders; and 6. low, smooth swing.

1. Grip

All great putters hold the club with their palms parallel, thumbs resting on top of the shaft. Though the actual grip may vary from reverse overlap to overlap to interlock to 10-finger, if a person is good at putting, you can always find his or her thumbs on top.

2. Balance

The way you set up to a putt should satisfy two requirements: First, you should feel solid and balanced over the ball. I've always liked watching the guys on the practice green who look as if you could kick them and it wouldn't sway them. Nicklaus and Watson come to mind. I'd suggest going through the same balance check with your putting stance that you did when preparing to take a full swing. Have a friend give you a light shove from all four sides at address. If you're easily swayed in any direction, you need to redistribute your weight. The best way to do that is to lower your center of gravity a little by crouching more, increasing knee flex, or combining both movements. Or, if you're toppled only laterally (by a push from the right or left side), widen your stance until you're more stable.

The second requirement that should be satisfied is that you feel comfortable over the ball and throughout the motion. Any discomfort is going to distract you from devoting complete concentration to making a good stroke and will also tend to result in a stroke that's manipulated with the hands and arms. Once again, there is no right or wrong way to go about finding a comfortable stance. What feels good to one golfer may feel awkward to another—it is simply a matter of personal preference. I can remember watching Palmer back in his heyday, when he would screw himself down into a knock-kneed,

... 4. **Eyes directly over the line, but not ahead of the ball**
5. **Square shoulders**
6. **Low, smooth swing**

pigeon-toed crouch, and I wondered how the heck that could feel comfortable. But Arnie sure rammed home his share of big putts when he had to with that stance. Jack Nicklaus is another one who prefers to get into a very compact, crouched position, while Ben Crenshaw and Bob Charles stand fairly erect.

A final word on comfort: if you have to adjust your putting stance for the sake of balance but you find the new position uncomfortable, my advice is to stick with it for a little while. Improving your balance is only going to help, not hurt, your putting, and one thing that will make any discomfort go away fast is to see the ball fall into the cup more often!

3. Steady Center

I talked about the importance of letting "center" shift in the full swing in order to ensure a complete weight shift. The end result of all that is maximum controlled clubhead speed. However, you can generate all the power you need for putting with the muscles of your hands, arms, and shoulders—there's no need to incorporate the legs, coil your body, or transfer your weight. Because of that, I believe it's better to keep the head still from the start of the backswing through impact, because it heightens the chances of returning the putterface squarely to the ball. Head and upper-body movement during the stroke will cause the clubhead path to waver, resulting in pushed or pulled putts. A common amateur error is to lift the head at impact, out of anxiety to see whether the ball is rolling on the intended line. Ironically, the very action of looking too quickly to see where the putt has gone is the cause for its being pushed or pulled off line. A good image to keep in mind is the long pendulum of a grandfather clock and the way it gently swings back and forth from an unmoving point at the top.

4. Eyes over the Line

Aiming a putt will be a whole lot easier if you address the ball and stroke it while looking straight down the target line, as you would to hit a cue ball in billiards or to fire a gun. Standing to the side of the ball as you do in golf makes it harder to tell whether the blade is aligned exactly perpendicular to the line on which you want to start the ball. And, as with full shots, being off by just a fraction can make a big difference in the outcome—often the difference between making a putt or lipping out.

The best view you can give yourself is by setting up with your

To find out if your eyes are over the ball, hold a second ball up to the bridge of your nose and let it drop straight down. If it drops on the first ball, your position is okay; if not, adjust your ball position until it does.

eyes directly over the ball or, if you like playing the ball farther forward in your stance toward your left foot, with your eyes over the line of the putt. To check where your eyes are in relation to the ball, first address a putt. Keeping your feet where they are, place two balls directly behind the first so all three form a straight line perpendicular to the clubface. Still keeping your feet stationary, drop the club behind you, crouch down into your putting stance, and hold a fourth ball up to the bridge of your nose. Gently release the ball so it drops straight down and see where it lands. If it comes down anywhere on top of the line of balls, then your eyes are in the best possible position from which to view the line of the putt, and they are not liable to play any tricks on you that will result in pushed putts (a sign the eyes are inside the line) or pulled putts (eyes are outside the line).

5. Square Shoulders

Good putters always set up with their shoulders square to the line on which they intend to start the ball out. Though not all keep their feet and hips square—Nicklaus and Crenshaw set up with theirs open— all keep their shoulders square to the line. If the shoulders slip open, you'll miss putts left, and right if they slip closed.

6. Low, Smooth Swing

The last fundamental has to do with the movement of the clubhead. Some people prefer to swing the putter with a long, smooth, flowing motion. Crenshaw immediately comes to mind. Other players prefer to make a short, compact backswing and "pop" the blade sharply through impact. Gary Player and Paul Azinger do this. Whichever way you prefer is okay, so long as you start the blade back smoothly and low to the ground and keep it low going through. That's a piece of advice Chandler Harper gave me when I was a teenager and it's been invaluable to me on the greens. You'll never see a good putter pick the blade up quickly with a jerk. Though players who use a pop stroke have a faster tempo than those with a flowing stroke, the start of the motion is (or should be) even and smooth.

There you have it: the six fundamentals present in every successful putting stroke. If you build them into yours, you're well on your way to becoming a good putter, if you aren't already.

MY STROKE

Although I said it was impossible to teach anyone the best way to stroke a putt because there is no "best" way, I'll still describe my stroke as I perceive it, since it may give you a few insights into your own.

I've always been lucky enough to have a consistently good putting game. I wouldn't call myself a great putter by any means, but I hole my share, and I have never suffered through any long periods of frustration that practice wouldn't have cured. There's no question that you've got to be a much-better-than-average putter to make it on tour. You've got to do more than just two-putt—you've got to make birdies to earn a living, and that means following up a good drive and approach by rolling the ball into the cup.

Ever since I started playing I've relied more on feel than on mechanical thoughts on the green. Not that I don't pay attention to

Though I prefer putting with my feet and hips open, my shoulders are always square to my target line.

mechanics: if my putting does take a turn for the worse, I immediately check the fundamentals previously covered, especially grip and alignment.

My personal preference is to set up with my feet and hips slightly open, shoulders square to my target line. I'd say that the amount of crouch I take is average, neither leaning toward low and compact nor straight and upright. Ball position is about one ball width forward of center, hands even with the ball. I'd advise against setting the hands ahead of the ball, since that creates negative loft on the putterface. Actually, although a putter appears not to have any loft (hence the nickname "flat stick"), it actually does have about two degrees. That little bit of upward angle is important to getting the ball rolling smoothly. If you tilt the clubhead forward and create a downward angle, you'll actually be pinching the ball slightly into the surface of the green at impact, possibly causing it to bounce off line. Because of the loft, you should have the feeling of hitting "down" on the ball instead of up.

Like many players, I prefer to use what's known as a reverse overlap grip to putt with. To take it, hold the club with your right little finger snugly against your left middle finger, laying the left index finger diagonally across the tops of the last three fingers of the right hand. Pressure on the grip is exerted mainly with the middle two fingers of the right hand and the last three fingers of the left. I like to think of them as being firmly on the club, but by no means tight. If my putting feel is poor, it's usually because I'm squeezing

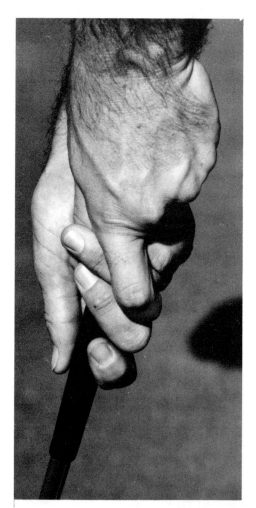 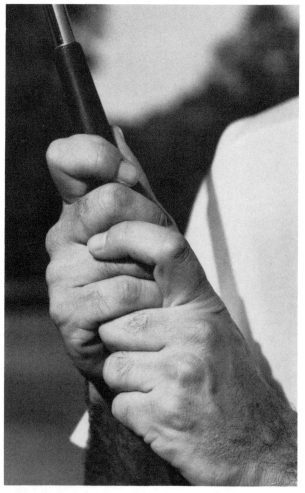

I prefer using the reverse overlap grip to putt. To take it, lay your left index finger in the valley formed between the middle and ring fingers of your right hand.

My main concern at address is to be balanced and comfortable, hands even with the ball.

Though I swing the putter using mainly my arms and shoulders, I do let my wrists cock slightly.

The putterhead should swing through like a pendulum, with the wrists "releasing" the club through impact and the putterhead continuing to move down the target line in the follow-through.

the club too hard, which chokes off the sensitivity you should be getting from your fingers.

I like the reverse overlap grip for putting because it allows my hands to work as a unit and stabilizes my left wrist so it doesn't break too much. My stroke is a combination of arms, shoulders, and wrists. You can see in the photos that as my arms and shoulders swing back, my wrists cock slightly. On the forward swing, the wrists uncock through impact, "releasing" the clubhead and squaring the face to the ball. Some players prefer to keep the wrists stiff throughout the stroke, but I've never liked that idea, nor would I recommend it. The

BERMUDA GRASS VS. BENT GRASS

Greens are usually composed of either bent grass or Bermuda grass, and the differences between them should be taken into account when putting. Bermuda grass blades are thick, so the direction they grow in (called the grain) will have a reasonable effect on the speed and break of the putt.

Bent grass, on the other hand, is much finer than Bermuda, so the surface tends to be quicker, especially when cut low. Because the blades are so fine, grain doesn't have much influence over the speed or break of the putt, which is why most people prefer playing on bent grass. Despite this, I think it's better for beginners to start out on Bermuda, because, in my opinion, it's harder to adjust to a surface where the grain has a definite effect on the putt than to a surface where grain has practically no effect.

smaller muscles in the hands, wrists, and forearms are where most of your feel is. Freezing them not only cuts down on some of the feel that's all-important in putting, but it also eliminates any release of the clubhead through impact, causing more mishit putts.

However, the reason I don't let the hands and wrists play a more dominant role, as they do in a very wristy stroke, is the same reason I don't want them to be too active in the full swing—the smaller the muscle, the more liable it is to get quick, twitchy, and jumpy under pressure, as opposed to the slow, steady pace of the larger muscles. That's why if I could, I would use the very biggest muscles of my legs and back to swing the putter, but since they lack feel, the compromise is to use the medium-sized muscles of the shoulders and arms, with the wrists coming into play just a little for the sake of feel. For me, this combination provides a certain degree of both touch and steadiness.

GREEN READING

Putting would be a lot simpler if every green were pool-table flat and smooth, but, of course, they aren't. Instead, we're faced with a number of variables that will influence the path the ball will take to the cup, and failure to take all of them into account can mean the difference between making or missing a putt, between hitting a good lag and three-putting. The variables that come into play are slope (uphill or downhill, right to left or left to right), surface speed, and sometimes grain direction. Each factor must be taken into consideration when assessing how a putt will roll.

Green reading should start before you reach the green if you're playing a course that's unfamiliar to you. As you approach the putting surface from the fairway, keep your eyes open to see which way it generally slopes, along with the terrain surrounding it. Usually it will be consistent with the nature of the rest of the land, but occasionally an architect will have done a little earth moving for the sake of drainage and added contouring. If so, it should be evident from a distance. This doesn't mean that every putt on that green is going to break in a particular direction, but the information may be useful later.

When I reach the green, I have a specific five-step preshot routine I perform before every putt, which fulfills two purposes, both of which are extremely important. One, it forces me to run through a checklist for gathering all the vital information I need to formulate a decision on how to get the ball into the cup: which way it will break and how hard to hit it. Second, by going through a familiar pattern

Green reading should start before you reach the surface. As you approach, check the general slope and character of the surrounding terrain for clues that might help you later.

of actions every time, I automatically fall into the proper frame of mind to focus all my attention on the task at hand, while shutting out outside distractions. That's important, especially under pressure situations—it allows me to keep my mind on making the putt, not missing it, or on getting it close, not letting it get away.

Step by step, here's my personal preputt routine. You'll find that it's pretty thorough, because I like to think of it more as stalking the putt instead of reading it, and I want to leave no stone unturned. My goal is to be so thorough that when I stand over the putt, everyone in the gallery will think I'm going to make it, which adds to my confidence.

Step #1—I squat down about five feet behind the ball and carefully scan the putting surface between the ball and cup, looking for clues of contour that will tell me which direction it's going to break. I look at the cup to see if it seems to slant in one direction or another, revealing which way the ground slopes. (Beware that although the ground around the cup may slope in one direction, there might also be a slant in the opposite direction somewhere in between the ball and the cup, giving you a double-breaking putt. On very undulating greens, you may find some long putts with three or even four different breaks.)

Step #2—I walk a few steps away from the line so that a triangular shape is formed between the cup, ball, and me. From this vantage point I can observe whether the slope is uphill or downhill. Usually that's pretty easy to determine, and if it's not, I know that it's basically flat; thus, speed won't be affected much one way or the other. It also gives me another view to help determine the way it will break.

Step #3—I reverse the first step by squatting behind the cup and looking toward the ball. By this time I hopefully have a good idea of how the putt will behave; if so, I'm merely checking whether what I see reconfirms that.

Step #4—I take a good, hard look around the cup and along the ground between the cup and ball, to fix any ball marks or irregularities that could throw the ball off track.

Step #5 (the final step)—I squat behind the ball and look toward the cup again, this time to plumb-bob. I'll do this even if I have already gotten a good idea of the existing conditions and how the putt will react to them, because it's part of my preputt routine, which I don't want to vary. Also, I may be interested in finding out what plumb-bobbing has to tell me if I still don't have a clear-cut idea of what's going to happen.

After plumb-bobbing, I picture the line the putt will take, and

A putt missed is a stroke gone forever.

PLUMB-BOBBING

When you see a player get behind a putt, dangle the puttershaft in front of his or her face, and squint toward the cup, he or she is "plumb-bobbing." Plumb-bobbing will *not* necessarily tell you which way a putt will break, but it *will* tell you in which direction the ground you're standing on slopes. The pitfall is that if the particular area where the cup is cut slopes in the opposite direction (as in double-breaking putts) and you don't realize it, you'll end up with a misread.

To plumb-bob, position yourself behind the ball so you can comfortably see both it and the cup, lining up so that your dominant eye forms a straight line with the ball and cup. (I like to squat down, though you can stand if you like.) Hold the putter loosely at the end of the grip so the shaft hangs straight down. Close one eye (not the dominant eye) and cover the ball with the shaft. If the cup appears on the left side of the shaft, the ground you're on slopes to the left; if the cup appears on the right, the ground slopes right; and if the cup is right behind the shaft, the ground is level.

Although plumb-bobbing is part of my normal putting routine, it's the last thing I do, so I've usually come to a decision about how the putt will break before getting to it. Still, I do it because it helps me relax and hopefully will reconfirm the decision I've made.

---

then I visualize the ball falling into the hole before taking address. Once I do, I take two practice strokes (no more, no less), address the ball, and stroke when I feel ready.

All that may sound like a lot of preparation, but it really goes fairly quickly if you move briskly from one step to another. Besides, I wouldn't dream of leaving out a single step, because, as I said at the beginning of this chapter, a putt missed is a stroke gone forever, so I want to do everything I can to get the ball into the cup, or as close as possible, because it is definitely elusive prey. Stats show that we pros actually miss more putts than we make from five feet and longer.

MAKE A DECISION AND STICK TO IT

Sometimes you'll get to the end of your preputt routine without getting a good idea of which way the putt is going to go. The only advice I can give you here is to decide on some kind of plan of action—right or wrong—and stick to it with confidence. It's my belief that most amateurs tend to make a tentative effort if they're unsure of what a putt is going to do. Look at it this way: even if it does come down to guesswork, if you guess correctly and make a good effort, you may sink the putt, but if you guess right and make a weak effort, you will never have a chance.

PUTTING STRATEGY

There are a couple of different ways to have a go at making a putt. "Charging" the cup means aiming for the back edge and trying to bounce the ball firmly off it and in. "Toppling" the ball in means hitting the ball at a soft enough speed so it will simply topple into the hole if it catches any part of the cup's edge.

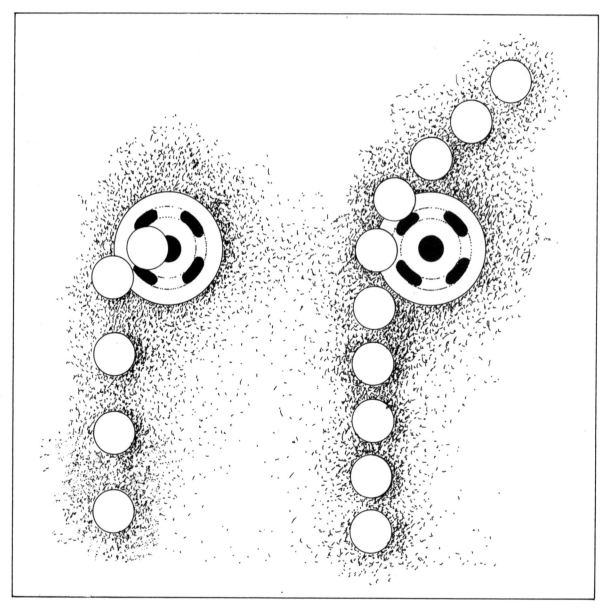

I prefer to roll my putts "softly" so that if the ball should happen to catch the edge, it will topple in (left), not lip out (right).

Charging is obviously the more aggressive route and was popularized back in the 1960s by Palmer. Arnold's slam-bang method of sinking putts was consistent with his "all or nothing" tee-to-green game. The advantage of charging is that it takes some of the break out of the putt—the harder you hit, the less the contour will affect it. Not many players cotton to this method, however, because the disadvantages seem to outweigh the advantages. For one, you're going to lip out more often when the ball is off center. And, of course, when you miss, you'll have more than a tap-in left. Arnold has said that the reason he was able to charge the cup with confidence in the old days was because he had so much faith in his ability to sink the four- or five-foot comebacker in case he missed. Another guy who putts very aggressively and sinks his share of testing second putts is Tom Watson.

I have always seen more advantages to toppling the ball into the cup. To me, it increases the size of the target; instead of zeroing in on just the back portion of the cup, you've got a larger area working for you. Short putts that are slightly pushed or pulled still have a good chance of catching a part of the edge and dropping in. Sure, I have to concentrate harder on reading the break and rolling the ball at a more precise speed, but I still think the odds of making it are better. Also, if I miss, there shouldn't be more than a tap-in left to finish, which I'd much rather have than a three- or four-footer to grind on.

If you choose the toppling strategy, don't fall into the trap of leaving putts short. The old saying "Never up, never in" still applies to toppling. To me, ideal speed will carry the ball three or four inches past the cup should it miss, but I never want to leave it short if it's a distance from which I think I can sink it.

How long should a putt be before you stop thinking about making it and start thinking about two-putting? Personally, I try to sink anything from 20 feet or less, regardless of conditions. From 20 to 30 feet I still try to sink the putt, but I'm not disappointed if I miss.

On putts of 30 feet and longer, you have to be realistic and just try to get down in two; that cup is a pretty small target from that distance, and to make it you have to have some luck on your side. On putts from a long distance I don't care if the ball comes up a little short of the cup; I just want to get it somewhere within three feet to cut the chances of three-putting. One of the oldest pieces of putting advice is to imagine a circle with a three-foot radius with the cup in the center. I guess some things work so well that they can't be improved upon, and this image is one of them. Use it and you'll get down in two (or even one) more often on very long putts.

To "topple" the ball into the hole, hit it just hard enough so that if it catches any part of the cup it will topple in instead of lipping out.

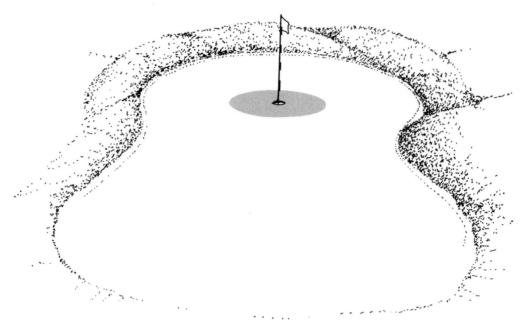

Make the target bigger on long lag putts by imagining a circle with a three-foot radius (six feet across) with the cup in the center.

SHORT PUTTS

Although a short putt (two- to six-foot range) may be the least physically demanding shot in golf, it's probably the most psychologically taxing. That's because when a putt is that short, you expect it to go in, and your playing partners expect it to go in. It doesn't matter if it's on a tricky sidehill or slick downhill slope; if it's a short putt, you know down deep that you're going to be irked if it doesn't drop. Nothing will make your stomach drop quite as fast as watching a three-footer (or less) burn the lip and stay out. Not only is it a stroke lost, it's embarrassing and frustrating.

Despite all that, you have to realize you can't make them all; we all miss from time to time. If you've ever watched tournament golf on television, you know that the pros, too, occasionally miss from short range (and we feel the same way about it that you do, believe me). Still, I feel you should never miss a short putt—if you start letting yourself off easy when you do, it's just going to lead to more misses.

The key to making short putts is confidence: if you miss two three-footers in a row, odds are good that your fear will snowball, leaving you scared to death of the next one. That's when you've got to have the guts to bear down and put a good stroke on it. The first short one you sink is the first step toward getting your confidence back.

SHARPENING THE EDGE OF YOUR PUTTING

Whether or not you're lucky enough to be a naturally good putter, it's a fact of golfing life that every player's green game is going to get a little stale from time to time. When it does, check first to make sure that the six key fundamentals are all healthy and intact. Besides that, you may find some help among the following drills and bits of advice that I've come across over the years. Bear in mind, though, that the best medicine is preventive—or, in other words, practice. I don't think *any* golfers practice their putting enough, especially amateurs.

Distance Dilemmas? Check Grip Pressure

Stroking the ball on the proper line is half the job; the other half is rolling it the right distance. Determining how hard to hit the ball gets more difficult as the putt gets longer. There's no doubt in my mind that more three-putt greens occur either from leaving the ball well short or running it too far past instead of poor line. If you find getting the right distance is difficult, check that your grip pressure isn't too tight, which will cut down on the amount of feel needed to gauge the speed of the stroke. Pay special attention to your index fingers, since both are very important to "feel," and squeezing too tightly will reduce their sensitivity.

Perfect Path Drill

Poor swing path on a full-swing shot can cause a push or pull. It can also cause a pushed or pulled putt. To groove a good, straight back-straight through path, take 30 golf balls and set them in two parallel rows of 15 each, just wide enough apart so you can rest your putter-head squarely in between with about half an inch to spare on either side. Place a ball in the middle and practice your stroke: the two rows of balls will force you to keep the putter on track.

You can also perform this drill by laying two clubs down so the shafts are parallel, but I prefer my way, since I'm less likely to get sloppy and more likely to concentrate on not upsetting either row of balls, because then I'd have to take the time to line them up carefully again.

A final variation on this drill is to take a striped range ball and set it down so the stripe lines up with your intended target line. Then roll the ball and keep your eye on the stripe. If it wobbles to one side or the other, it means you're cutting across the ball from either the inside or outside. Adjust your path until you can consistently make the stripe roll straight.

SPIKE MARKS
A spike mark is an irregularity on the putting surface caused by a spike on a golf shoe. Although it's legal to fix ball marks (caused sometimes when a ball lands on a green with enough force to damage the surface), it's illegal to fix spike marks before putting. So if a spike mark is in your intended line, you have to accept it as a rub of the green. The only time it's legal to fix spike marks is after everyone in your group has putted out. After your group is finished do the players behind you a favor by tamping down any spike marks with the sole of your putter. (I was always taught to leave the course in better condition than I found it if I could, and this is one way of doing that.) If you accidentally make one yourself, fix it immediately so you don't forget.

To groove a good swing path, line up two rows of golf balls and practice swinging the putterhead between them.

Alignment Aid: Short Putts

A drill I use when I have problems with aiming is to find a straight two-footer on the practice green and putt it over and over and over, hitting literally hundreds of putts. Because it's such a short distance, you can see the hole, ball, and stroke all at once, and you don't have to worry much about how hard to hit it, leaving you free to concentrate on aiming the putterhead and rolling the ball straight. Besides that, you know immediately if the putt started on line (it will go straight in) or if it didn't (it won't). When your confidence is rock-solid from two feet, increase to four. If you want, place a ball marker halfway between the cup and ball as an intermediate target when you increase the length.

A good cure for poor putterface alignment is to practice dozens and dozens of two-footers.

Strike the Sweet Spot

Constantly leaving putts short of the cup is a sign that you aren't striking the ball solidly. The first thing to do is find exactly where the sweet spot is. Take the putter by the very end of the grip in one hand and let it dangle freely. With your other hand, tap the clubface lightly with the edge of a coin until you find the point where the clubhead rebounds straight back instead of twisting to the left or right. That is the sweet spot—mark it clearly. (Try this test even if the manufacturer has already put a mark on the putter, since these marks aren't always placed accurately.)

When you putt, turn the label on the ball so it lines up with the target line. Then try to meet the label with the sweet-spot mark. You'll make more solid and satisfying contact with the ball, and put a better roll on it.

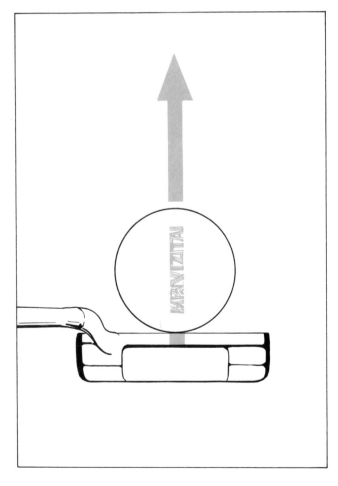

Find the sweet spot: the point where the clubhead rebounds straight back instead of twisting to the left or right.

Line up the label on the ball with the target line; then try to meet the label with the sweet spot.

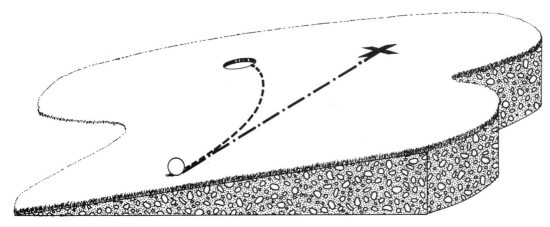

To force yourself to play enough break on severely breaking putts, forget about the cup and concentrate on a secondary target.

Big Breakers: Forget the Cup

Once in a while you're going to run into a putt with a lot of break—maybe five or six feet. When there's this much bend involved, it isn't very realistic to expect to make the putt; the best you can usually hope for is to get it close. When I have a putt like that, I first imagine the line I think the putt will take, starting at the ball and finishing in the side of the hole. Then I forget about the cup and pick something else to aim the putterface at to make sure that I get the ball started on the line I want. It might be something actually on the green, like an old ball mark, or something in the distance, like a tree—anything that I can use as reference and toward which I can get the ball moving. Once I've picked a target, all I have to do is figure how hard to hit it and stroke—the heavy contour will do the work of bringing the ball back to the hole.

I think most recreational players would benefit a lot from this trick, even on putts that break two or three feet, because they often have a tendency to mistrust that the slope will bring the ball back to the hole, and they end up pulling the putterhead from outside in on putts that break sharply from right to left or pushing it inside out if the putt goes left to right. The result is that the ball breaks well below the hole.

Makeable Breakers: Imagine a Side Door

Maybe you've heard the terms "pro side" and "amateur side" in putting. The story goes that most of the time amateurs don't read enough break, so the ball ends up breaking below the cup and never having a chance to go in. If a pro misses, he will most likely err to the far side by reading too much break (so the story goes). Either way, the end result is the same since neither putt goes in, but the pro is supposed to take some satisfaction in the fact that his had a chance, where the amateur's didn't.

I think most amateurs leave makeable breaking putts short because they focus on the front portion of the cup, thus making the target smaller. If the ball is breaking in from one side or the other, then imagine it dropping in the side of the cup, not catching the front edge. Try this and see if it doesn't make a difference.

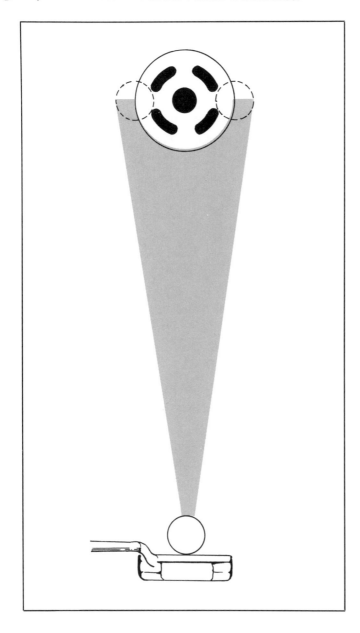

On putts of three feet and closer, don't aim outside the edges of the cup. You'll find that if you stick to this rule, you'll make more of these "testers" and very rarely will the ball break below the hole.

Short Putts: Don't Give the Hole Away

When you're advised not to "give the hole away," it means not to aim outside the right or left edge of the cup. That's a good rule on any putt of about three feet and less, because the ball usually won't have enough time to break more than a couple of inches before it reaches the cup. If you aim for the right edge and the ball breaks two inches left, it's in the center. If it goes straight, it will still catch the edge and drop in (provided you hit it easy enough). Break this rule only when the sidehill slope is really great or if the surfaces are ultrafast (for example, I'll usually waive it at the Masters, where the greens are very fast).

CHOOSING A PUTTER THAT'S RIGHT FOR YOU

Just as putting style and strategy should be dictated by personal preference, so should the type of putter you choose. What feels and works fine for player A may not appeal at all to player B. Although I can't tell you what kind of putter will work best for you, I can list the qualities that I look for.

Alignment

First, I check to see that the face stays square to the target line when I rest it behind the ball—some putterheads will fall into an open or closed position if you hold them very lightly at address, and I recommend avoiding any putter that does this, because it means the lie doesn't match well with your address position.

Balance

If the balance is correct for your needs, the putter will almost feel as if it swings back and through by itself—you won't feel as if it's twisting or as if you're fighting its movement in any way. Balance depends upon the weight distribution from heel to toe, the putter's total weight (including the shaft), and your level of strength. A putter that feels nicely balanced to a 200-pound man may feel heavy to a 90-pound woman.

Length

If you prefer to crouch very low, you may need a shorter shaft than average, but beware that cutting the length of an existing shaft may affect the club's overall balance.

Lie

I've always felt that amateurs should make sure that the sole of their putter lies flat on the ground when they address the ball. However, there are some tour players who are excellent putters who tilt the toe up in the air—Isao Aoki and Seve Ballesteros, to name two. These guys have practiced long hours that way; most weekend players don't. To me, the dangers of catching the bottom of the club on the ground and mishitting the putt are too high, especially if you don't play that often. You'll put a good roll on the ball much more consistently if you use a putter that rests flat and clean when you take your address. If you prefer to hold your hands a little farther from your body than normal, you'll need a more upright lie. If you feel better with your hands closer to your body, you need a flatter lie. Make sure when you choose, though, that your eyes are over the line.

Being a good putter takes guts.

HEART: IT MEANS MORE THAN MECHANICS

A lot of guys with great strokes aren't great putters because they never had the nerve to be.

Tom Weiskopf, a former tour pro, said that, and I agree with it wholeheartedly. It all goes back to what I said at the very beginning of this chapter—being a good putter takes guts. If I were playing a team match and my partner had a six-footer to win for us on the last green, I'd rather have on my side a player with only a mediocre stroke but who I knew was mentally tough, instead of someone who had great stroke mechanics but wasn't known for the ability to bear down. There are some people who may not rank in the top 25 in putting stats, but pressure situations bring out the best in them—they simply have what it takes. When you come right down to it, two things can happen: you make it or you miss it. If you're afraid you're going to miss, you probably will, so forget everything and concentrate only on getting the ball into the hole. Mechanics are important, but when it gets down to the nitty-gritty, it's heart that sets those mechanics in motion and gets the ball into the cup.

7
TROUBLE PLAY:
GET OUT OF JAIL FREE

If you play golf, you're going to hit the ball into trouble once in a while, so you may as well adopt a good attitude toward getting out, instead of grumbling about it. The best way to handle trouble is certainly to stay out of it, but because physical mistakes are bound to happen, don't get overly upset if you spray one off the beaten track once in a while. In this chapter you can bone up on the proper technique needed to get out of just about any trouble situation you're apt to run into.

ROUGH

Rough is the most common form of trouble found on any course. You may encounter a hole here and there that doesn't feature any sand or water hazards, but there's practically always going to be some long grass bordering either side of the fairway from tee to green. How much of a problem it poses depends on how much resistance it creates for the clubhead, which depends on a number of factors: height, thickness, lushness, direction, and lie.

Sometimes you've got to roll up your sleeves (and pants) and work to save par.

Height

The higher the grass, the more resistance it poses. The rough at Augusta National isn't considered much of a hazard, since it's traditional not to let it grow very high. (The officials figure that the fast, tricky greens, water hazards, and overall length of the course give the players enough to contend with.) Just the opposite is the U.S. Open and the PGA Championship, where the rough is allowed to grow high, posing a severe penalty for a missed fairway or green. It's often so deep that a ball may disappear from sight unless you're right on top of it.

Thickness

Thickness depends on how dense the growth is where the ball lies. If the number of blades is relatively sparse, they won't do much to slow down or impede a speeding clubhead. However, if the grass is indeed thick, it will form a firm barrier between the ball and the clubface. Of all types of grass, Bermuda is the thickest.

Lushness

What I mean by lushness is how healthy is the grass? Blades that are dry and brittle offer less resistance than grass that is strong and green. During the very hot, dry summer months most courses won't waste water on the rough, allowing it to dry out.

Always take a practice swing to get a feel for the resistence.

Direction

Usually rough won't seem to be growing in any particular direction except up, but when it's very long it will sometimes lean in one general direction. If the grass is growing toward the target, the clubhead will slide through more easily than if it's growing in any other direction. Bluegrass usually grows in one pronounced direction.

Lie

When I say "lie," I am referring to how deeply in the grass the ball is nestled. This is important, since a ball perched on top of thick, high grass can be struck cleanly and advanced much farther than a ball that has sunk down deep.

If the ball is perched on top, choke down on the grip a little; then stand a little straighter at the knees and hips and measure yourself to the ball. Take care at address that you don't disturb the ball and cause it to fall deeper into the grass—not only will you have a tougher lie, but it's also a one-stroke penalty if the ball moves after you've addressed it.

These are the factors that contribute to how much resistance the rough will be. The more factors that are against you, the harder it will be to get the ball out. Always take a practice swing to get a feel for the resistance—if the grass grabs hold of the club you intend to use

Hover the clubhead to avoid disturbing a ball perched in high grass.

Long irons work poorly from rough because their shallow, sweeping downswing paths force them to fight through a lot of grass. Short irons are a better choice because of their steeper downswing angle.

and stalls it, you'd better make a different choice. The rough on most of the courses we play on tour is fairly difficult, and I've seen plenty of my pro-am partners playing out of it. The biggest mistake I've observed among them and the pros in general is that they try to do more with the shot than the lie will allow. Accept the fact that if the lie is very difficult, you may have to back down to a shorter-shafted club and play a shorter shot, even if it means not reaching the green. The most important thing is to get the ball back into play instead of leaving it in trouble. I'd much rather get the ball out of the rough and near the green with a chance to get up and down for par than risk hitting a very poor shot from the high grass. The shorter the club-shaft, the easier it is to get out of the rough, because the swing arc is not as wide, resulting in a more descending blow. The clubhead doesn't have to fight through as much grass as it would if the approach path were longer and shallower. Another advantage is that the shorter the shaft, the more loft the club has, giving it a sharper leading edge, which helps it cut through the grass easier. That's why you'll sometimes see a player, especially during the U.S. Open or PGA, simply take a pitching wedge and get the ball back onto the fairway; with any other club he knows that the chances are good that he may not be able to hack the clubhead through the long grass and may leave the ball there.

Normally, the average player isn't going to run into conditions so severe that a wedge is the only choice for getting out of the rough. However, if the lie prohibits a long iron, consider a 4- or 5-wood; the smooth, rounded head will slide easily through moderate rough to sweep the ball out without tangling in it.

The Flier

Even when rough is not particularly high or thick, it still presents a problem. The trickiest part about playing an approach shot from light or moderate rough is determining how far the ball will go. The grass intervening between the ball and clubface cuts down on the amount of backspin put on the ball, so it flies higher and longer than usual. (Moisture can also cause this to happen.) How *much* longer can be hard to estimate. Also, because it has less backspin, the ball will run when it lands, instead of checking up and stopping quickly. This means that even if you do land the ball on the green, it may not hold the surface. Pros call this kind of shot a "flier" or "jumper," and they back down a club or two when it appears that the shot is going to behave this way. Its unpredictability is one of the hazards of the rough and a good reason to keep the ball in the fairway.

Exploding from Heavy Green-Side Rough

If green-side rough is very heavy, I'd rather miss the green by hitting into a bunker than into the high grass—again because how the ball will react is unpredictable. The clubhead may happen to slide through the grass easily, popping the ball out quickly, or it may get bogged down and barely get the ball out. So much grass coming between the clubface and ball makes it difficult to judge the reaction.

When I'm faced with a shot like this, I play it like an explosion from sand, with an open stance and open sand wedge, hitting down firmly just behind the ball. What happens is that the grass between the club and ball compresses together and acts like a cushion, and the force of the clubhead drives this cushion into the ball and forces it up and out. Of course, it's hard to be precise with this shot—getting it close is due more to luck than skill—but through practice you can develop a certain amount of feel for the shot and for the resistance the high grass will present.

To "explode" from heavy green-side rough, open your sand wedge and hit down firmly an inch behind the ball, as you would when exploding from sand.

WIND PLAY

Wind can be a form of trouble if it's strong enough to have an effect on the flight of the ball. Playing in high wind will really test your patience, since it can certainly make a big difference in the distance and direction the ball goes, making the process of aiming and club selection a lot more difficult than usual. I personally pay special attention to the direction and strength of the wind at all times, since I know it can mean the difference between hitting or missing a fairway or green.

Headwinds

Wind in your face is going to cut the distance of the shot; how much depends on how hard the wind is blowing. The most common mistake amateurs make when playing into the wind is to swing too hard, which usually results in a mishit. Instead, you should accept the fact that the shot is going to play longer and take more club and, above all, concentrate on making solid contact.

The ball is going to climb higher and land shorter, so you'll need more club; how much more depends on how hard the wind is blowing. I may go up as many as three or even four clubs if the wind is very stiff.

Another way to reduce the effect of a headwind is by hitting the ball lower, "under" the wind. Suppose I have a 9-iron to the green, but a 1-club wind is blowing in my face. Then, I may take the 9-iron and play the ball back in my stance, taking some of the loft off the club so the ball flies lower. This is known as a "knockdown" shot. If

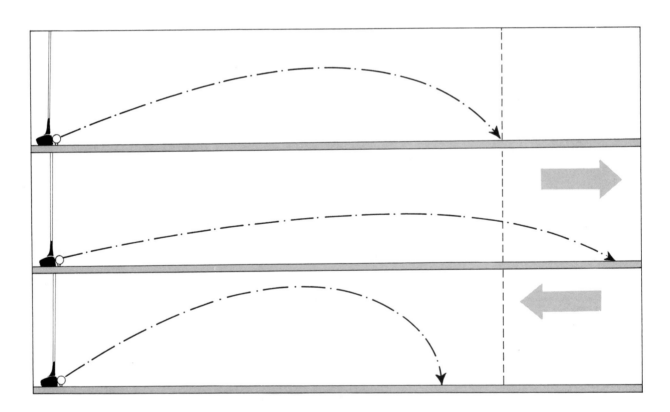

A tail wind (center) will give you more distance but will also take backspin off the ball, causing it to fly lower and run more after landing. A head wind (bottom) will make the shot fly higher and land shorter, coming down on a steep angle that results in little roll.

the wind is very strong, I may take more club, say an 8- or 7-iron, and still play a knockdown. When playing this type of shot, remember to swing easy: the easier you hit the ball, the lower it will go.

Tailwinds

A wind at your back is great off the tee, because it can give you more distance. Beware, though, that a tailwind will "push" the ball, taking the spin off it and causing it to come down on a shallower angle than usual and run after landing. These factors can be tricky when approaching a green. It's just as important to drop down a club or more with the wind behind you; otherwise, you'll end up running past or flying over your target. Again, the lower you keep the ball, the more control you'll have over it.

Crosswinds

I only have one rule of thumb for playing crosswinds, and that is to let the wind work the ball for me. The only way you'll find out how much it affects the ball flight is through experience, but remember that the lower you keep the ball, the less it will be affected by the breeze.

SLOPING LIES

Golf was invented in Scotland back in the 15th century; the first courses were laid out by sheepherders according to the rolling lay of the land along the Scottish shoreline. Perfectly flat lies were rarely encountered because of the character of the terrain. Over the years, golf-course construction benefited from the advancement of heavy earth-moving equipment; still, you won't find many courses that have been smoothed flat, because playing off different slopes is yet another challenge of golf. Sloping ground is something like the wind—if the angle is slight, it doesn't pose much of a problem and can be pretty much ignored. But if there's a great deal of slope involved, then, like a strong wind, it will have an effect on the shot and is something you must compensate for.

Uphill

If the lie is uphill, make sure to set the lines of your knees, hips, and shoulders parallel to the slope, your weight evenly distributed. Guard against unconsciously flexing your left knee too much to compensate

When your left foot is higher than your right, make sure that your knees, hips, and shoulders are parallel to the slope.

for the slope. Keep the right leg firm and braced, though, and the weight on the inside of the right foot.

Beware that because the slope tilts upward, the shot will naturally fly higher and shorter than from a flat lie, depending on how severe the slope is.

Downhill

Set knees, hips, and shoulders parallel to the slope, letting the degree of slope distribute your weight more toward your left side. Downhill

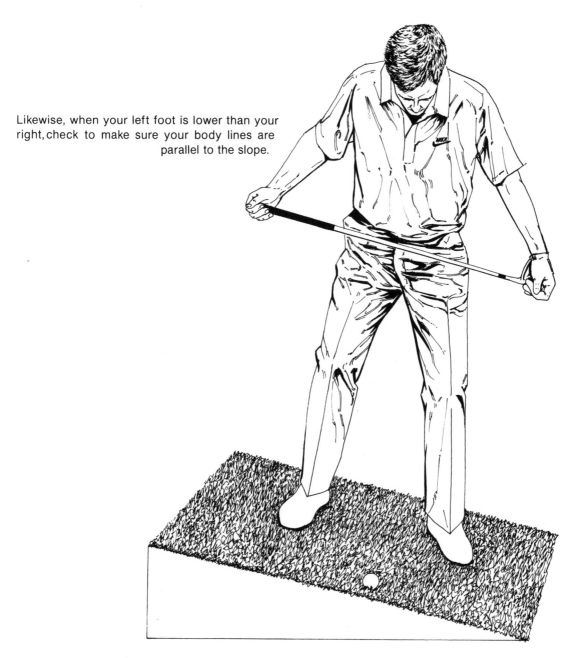

Likewise, when your left foot is lower than your right, check to make sure your body lines are parallel to the slope.

lies are fat shots waiting to happen; to prevent that, play the ball back about half of a ball width. Also, concentrate on swinging the clubhead back low along the angle of the slope on the takeaway to avoid picking up the club too abruptly and chopping down behind the ball.

The downward angle of the slope will cause the ball to fly lower and shorter. Clubs with less loft—fairway woods and long irons—will be harder to hit, so concentrate on staying down and through and don't try to help the ball in the air.

You'll have to stand farther from the ball with straighter posture than usual when the ball is above your feet, forcing a flatter swing plane.

Ball Above the Feet

When the slope is such that the ball is above your feet, it forces you to stand farther from the ball and swing on a flatter plane than usual. The flatter plane will cause ball flight to move from right to left; how much depends on how flat you're forced to swing. A ball well above your feet is going to have a pretty good-sized hook on it. To keep from hitting the shot fat, make a mental note of how much the slope allows you to bend at the waist at address, and maintain this spine angle throughout the swing. Measure yourself to the ball at address and make sure you're connected at address. Keep in mind also that you'll have a better chance of hitting the ball solid with a shorter-shafted club because of the clubhead control.

Ball Below the Feet

When the ball lies below the level of your feet, you have to bend more at the waist and knees than usual to address it; this forces a more upright swing plane that results in a left-to-right ball flight. Again, how much the ball bends depends on how far below your feet it is. Obviously, the longer the shaft, the less you have to flex to get the clubhead down to the ball, so the easier the shot will be. To prevent topping, key in on the amount of knee flex and spine angle you feel at address and try to maintain it on the downswing and through impact. Avoid letting your weight move too much toward your toes, and use a little less body movement and more arms when you swing.

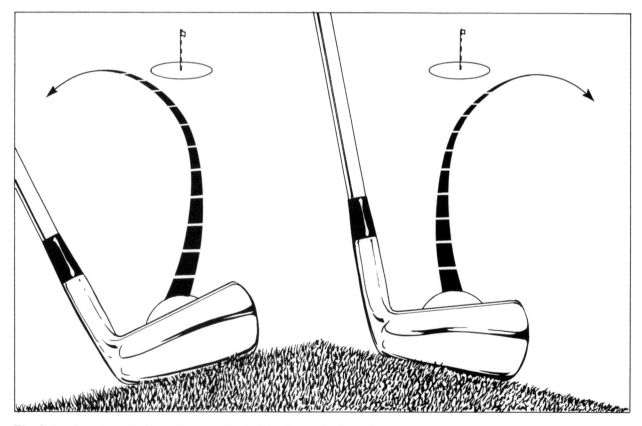

The flat swing plane that results when the ball is above the feet will cause the ball to fly from right to left. Likewise, the upright plane resulting from a ball below the feet equals a left-to-right ball flight.

A ball below your feet will force you to stand closer to the ball and bend more at the waist, forcing a more upright swing plane.

FAIRWAY SAND

Exploding from green-side sand is an effective way to play the shot because distance isn't much of a factor. But when the ball lies in a fairway bunker 150 yards from the green, there's no way anyone could hit an explosion that far. To put distance on the shot, you can't allow any sand to get between the ball and club, deadening impact, so you have to alter your technique in order to pick the ball cleanly.

Because you *have* to hit the ball first, play it back one-half of a ball width from normal. How you take your stance is important, since the loose sand doesn't provide much stability unless you dig your feet down in a little, but don't overdo it. For added stability, angle the soles of your shoes inward slightly. Concerning posture, stand slightly straighter at the hips and knees, hovering the clubhead behind the ball. Since you have to make precise contact, clubhead control is more important than clubhead speed, so I usually take one more club than usual and make a three-quarter swing, concentrating hard on keeping my right shoulder and hip level on the downswing. If you're going to mishit this shot, it's better to be thin than fat.

When choosing a club, remember that you'll lose some height on the shot by playing the ball back, so make sure whatever you select has enough loft to get the ball over the front lip. This may force you into laying up short of the target, but that's part of the penalty for hitting into the trap. However, despite the fact that a high lip may limit you to a high-lofted club, there's no reason not to go with a long iron or even a fairway wood if the lip allows, so long as the lie is flat and clean. (See fairway sand shot illustration on next page.)

OUT OF A DIVOT HOLE

If you've ever cracked a tee shot right where you wanted it only to find it sitting in a divot hole left by a careless player, you know what the word *frustrated* means. Fortunately, it's a pretty rare occurrence, but because it can happen, you should know how to handle the situation. It's simple, really—just play the ball about one-half of a ball width behind normal, to make sure of hitting the ball first with a descending blow. The shot will fly low and land without bite. Avoid fairway woods and long irons from this kind of lie, which require low, sweeping downswings—I recommend using nothing more than a 4-iron to cut the chances of smothering the ball.

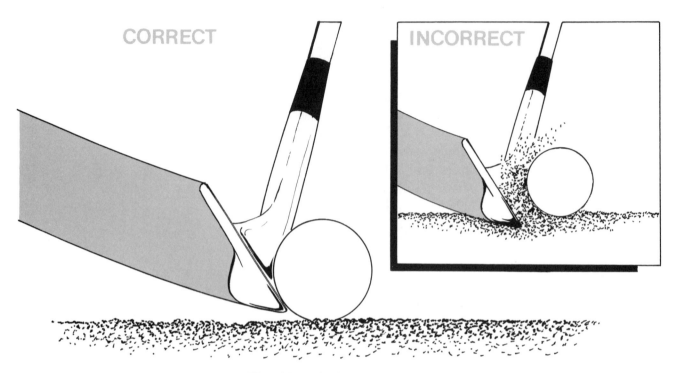

The object of a fairway sand shot is to hit the ball first; trapping any sand in between the clubface and ball will ruin the shot.

OUT OF THE WATER

A ball hit into a water hazard won't always end up unplayable, if you have the nerve to go for it. Hitting a water shot is definitely a messy undertaking and never easy, but I won't shy away from it if it means saving a stroke. Whether you decide to attempt it should depend solely on the lie. Try only if some part of the ball is protruding above the water's surface. If it's completely submerged, accept the penalty and take a drop. The reason for this is because you have to play it like an explosion from sand, hitting behind the ball hard to move it and the water immediately surrounding it. If the ball is completely underwater, that means you've got to move a lot of water, and you will probably end up leaving the ball in the drink—and getting a face full of water on top of it.

If the ball is indeed playable, take a pitching wedge and set up open (you may want to take one shoe off). Clubface should be square, with your hands ahead of it so that the face is angled downward a little, helping it slice smoothly through the water instead of flopping into it. Pick up the club sharply with your right hand and hit down about two inches behind the ball, concentrating on knifing the clubhead cleanly through the water and to the ball. Your main concern is to get the club under the ball. Hit hard, since water puts up a lot of resistance and there's a much bigger chance of leaving it in the hazard than hitting it way too far.

Probably the toughest part of playing from the water is forcing yourself to stay down on the shot through impact without flinching. Expect to get wet.

Expect to get wet!

8
EVERYTHING YOU NEED TO
KNOW ABOUT SAND PLAY

Some football coaches don't like to throw the forward pass because they figure that out of the three things that are likely to happen—an interception, an incompletion, or a completion—two of them are bad. Too many amateurs carry that same poor attitude with them into sand traps. Most figure that they'll either leave the ball in the bunker, accidentally pick it clean and knock it clear over the green, or, last and least likely, get it safely onto the putting surface. This kind of negative thinking doesn't do much to help them pull off the shot.

When I face a green-side sand shot, I imagine three possible things that can happen: 1. good shot, make a short putt for par; 2. fair shot, make a good putt for par; and 3. poor shot, make a great putt for par. No matter what happens, I envision making par, while most amateurs envision the worst.

Another reason I think many amateurs in this country are afraid of sand is because most don't really understand how a sand wedge works and what exactly happens when a ball is correctly "exploded" out. I say "this country" because in Japan you'll rarely see a really poor bunker player among nonprofessionals, mainly because you rarely see poor bunker technique. Over here, I can usually spot a shaky sand player before he or she hits the shot by the poor technique displayed at address. Tipoffs include a strong grip, closed stance, closed clubface, and playing the ball back in the stance.

In this chapter I'll teach you what actually happens during an "explosion" shot and demonstrate how a sand wedge is designed to work. With that knowledge and a little practice on your side, any "attitude" problems you may have should take care of themselves.

WHAT HAPPENS DURING AN "EXPLOSION"?

The term "explosion" comes from the fact that when the shot is properly played, a cloud of sand is raised. That's because the object is to hit intentionally behind the ball, moving the sand and taking the ball with it.

The reason it's better to explode the ball than to try to pick it cleanly off the surface is because "picking" allows no margin for error: Hit behind just a little and sand will be scooped up onto the clubface, deadening the impact and keeping the ball from springing off the club—the consequence is that the ball is almost always left in the trap. The opposite extreme is to hit the ball thin, so it flies low and probably into the lip. Again, the ball will probably stay in the hazard.

On an explosion shot from sand, the club slides under the ball, displacing the sand that the ball rests on and the ball with it.

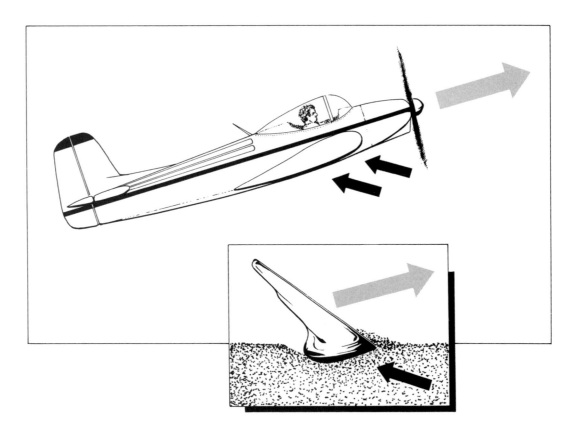

Instead of risking either of these results, it's better to hit intentionally behind the ball and "explode" it out, swinging harder to compensate for the cushioning effect of the sand. The main thing to remember is that the object is to hit behind the ball so you can get the club *underneath* it.

The large flange of a sand wedge works similarly to an airplane wing: pressure on the bottom combined with the upward angle forces the clubhead up and out of the sand.

How a Sand Wedge Works

Green-side sand play was revolutionized in 1931 by one of the greatest golfers in history, Gene Sarazen, who invented the sand wedge.

The idea behind the sand wedge came to Sarazen while he was taking flying lessons; he learned that what makes an airplane climb into the air is that the wings are tilted slightly upward, and the pressure of onrushing air under them lifts the plane up. He decided to apply that idea to a wedge. Using solder, he enlarged the flange of a regular pitching wedge and rounded the leading edge slightly. Then, by opening the face of the club, the angle of the big flange slanted upward, similar to the angle of an airplane wing. So by opening the clubface and driving it down into the sand, he found that the angle of the large flange would drive it upward and back out of the sand, instead of digging farther downward and getting mired. Sarazen found that the more he opened the blade and increased the angle of the flange, the easier the club would bounce through.

The sand wedge had an immediate impact. Sarazen took it to the 1932 British Open at Sandwich, used it exceptionally from the sand, and took the title by five shots. Two weeks later, he won his second U.S. Open at Fresh Meadows Country Club in New York.

Playing the Explosion

The way that I, and most of my peers on tour, play explosion shots doesn't differ much from the way Sarazen did.

First, I set up in an open stance, digging my feet in just enough for stability, with my weight about 60 percent on the inside of my left foot. The clubface should be open and aimed slightly right of my target line. Remember, you're going to hit behind the ball, so instead of addressing the ball, imagine a line in the sand behind the ball where you want the club to make contact and address that, playing it just forward of center.

My own preference is to hit about an inch and a half behind the ball for most green-side sand shots, varying the force of my swing according to how far I want the ball to go. Some players like to hit a little closer behind the ball, but I prefer an inch and a half for a few reasons: 1. If I'm off the mark a little bit toward the near side of the ball, there still isn't any danger of accidentally picking the ball clean and sending it over the green; 2. If I miss the mark slightly to the far side of the ball, I won't be in danger of taking so much sand that the ball won't clear the lip of the hazard; 3. I like my bunker shots to have as little spin as possible—like a knuckleball. As you may have observed in your own explosion shots or in those of someone else, you can put a great deal of backspin on a sand shot; how much depends on how little sand you take and how close the club hits behind the ball. Hitting an inch-and-a-half behind results in little or no spin on the shot.

When I swing back, I want to think about picking the clubhead up quickly with my hands by making a fast wrist cock with the small muscles of my hands and wrists, resulting in a very steep up-and-down swing plane. (If the downswing angle is too shallow, the clubhead will skid off the surface without digging in at all, so the leading edge makes contact with the middle of the ball, "bellying" it forward on a hard, low line of flight.) The more you open the face and the steeper the angle on which you swing down, the higher the ball will fly and the softer it lands.

The downswing should be smooth and controlled, but don't be shy—release the clubhead down hard without trying to help the ball

To play a basic explosion shot, start by opening two things—your stance and the clubface—while keeping grip position the same as usual.

into the air. The clubhead will dig down under the ball before the angle of the flange forces it up and out of the sand, sending the sand and the ball it rests on up and out. At impact, I want my right hand to pass my left, but not to roll over it. To do that, you have to let your left wrist cup as you swing through impact.

To summarize: Open your stance and the clubface; cock your wrists quickly with the small muscles on the backswing; then hit down briskly behind the ball. The blade will dig under the ball; then the angle of the flange will guide the clubhead upward and out of the sand, taking the ball with it.

At address, the ball should be just forward of center, with about 60 percent of your weight on the left side.

Here you should put the small muscles to work—cock your wrists quickly on the backswing, swinging the club back using mainly your arms.

Hit down sharply about an inch and a half behind the ball, the object being to let the clubhead dig down underneath the ball, displacing both ball and the sand on which it lies.

The clubface should pass your hands, but
remain open through impact so that it faces
the sky in the follow-through. . . .

. . . If you let the toe pass the heel,
the shot will fly low and hard instead
of high and soft.

A view from down-target: here you can see how open my stance is in relation to my target, the pin.

This angle also shows how steep the backswing plane should be; the shaft points nearly straight up.

Gauging Distance

There are two ways to gauge how far an explosion shot goes. The first is to keep the distance you hit behind the ball constant and simply vary the force of your swing. The second way is to vary the amount of sand you take. The closer behind the ball you hit, the less sand you take and thus the farther the ball will go. The farther you hit behind the ball, the more sand you take, so the shot won't go as far.

I like the first method best, and I recommend it to amateurs. It's much simpler and easier to be consistent by taking the same amount

Again, hit down briskly into the sand and follow through with the clubface toward the sky, and the ball will float up and over the lip.

of sand every time, and you don't have to worry about taking too much or none at all.

The only time I deviate from this rule is when I want to make a very short explosion—say, to carry the ball only eight or 10 feet. Then I'll address the same imaginary line just forward of center, but with the ball a little farther forward than usual. Next, I open the face a little more than usual, and I make a point to release very hard. By playing the ball a little farther forward, I take a little more sand, allowing me to swing aggressively and still not be in danger of hitting the ball well past the pin.

Long Bunker Shots

Occasionally your ball will wind up in a trap that's close to the green, but not exactly green-side—maybe 20 or 30 yards away. Getting that ball close to the pin is one of the hardest shots in golf, mainly because it's tough enough to be distance-accurate on a regular pitch shot in that range, let alone trying to explode the ball. Whenever I get one of these shots close to the hole, I know that luck had a little to do with it—normally I'm happy to get within 10 feet.

There are a couple of ways to play this shot. The way I do it is to take some of the loft of the wedge by squaring the face up so it's just a hair open, using a normal (not upright) swing by closing my stance so it, too, is only a little open. I'll also hit just about a half an inch closer behind the ball, so I take only an inch of sand. Along with these adjustments, I vary swing force depending on the length of the shot.

The second way to play a very long explosion is the way my friend Greg Norman does it. Greg maintains the same very open stance and

To play a high, short explosion, the clubface should be open. (left) To play a longer, lower shot, square the clubface and keep the rest of your technique the same.

clubface he uses for green-side explosions, but he gets more distance using more club—PW, 9-iron, 8-iron, etc., depending on how far he wants the shot to go. However, to make up for the smaller flange on these clubs, he has to hit very close behind the ball, which is why I don't recommend this method to amateurs, nor do I do it myself. If you should try it, beware that the ball will come out low and running, so make sure you have plenty of green to work with.

HARD DAYS AT THE BEACH

Getting out of sand gets a little tougher when you don't have a clean, flat lie. Here's how to handle some of the more "interesting" bunker lies you're liable to run into.

Buried Lies

A shot that's hit very high and lands directly in a trap on a steep angle will sometimes bury if the sand is soft enough, meaning that the bottom of the ball has burrowed a certain amount below the top of the bunker's surface. A ball that's semiburied is better known as a "fried egg" because that's what it looks like. A ball that is deeper down in the sand so that all or nearly all of it is covered has no cute nickname; it's called, simply, a buried ball. Here are the techniques I use to get out of these sandy graves.

Fried Egg

Because the ball is sitting in a small crater, the bottom of which is deeper than the surface of the trap, you've got to dig down deeper and

Square the clubface to remove the ball from a "fried egg" lie.

SAND ETIQUETTE

Never ground (touch the sand) with the clubhead at address. A sand trap is a hazard, and grounding the club in it is a two-stroke penalty.

If one side of the trap is higher than the other, *always* enter it from the lower side; coming in from the high side will cause sand to slide off the steep face to the bottom of the trap.

Always rake the trap after playing out, or at least smooth it with the back of your sand wedge if no rake is available. Poor lies in sand are frustrating enough, especially when un-called for. In a professional tournament, it's the responsibility of the caddy to smooth the bunker out so that it is as it was before the player entered it. This is considered so important that a fine will be levied against any caddy who doesn't do so.

move more sand with the clubhead than when exploding from a flat lie. Your best bet is to use a sand wedge and close the face a little at address. The closed face (which decreases the effective bounce) will allow the club to slice down far enough to get completely under the ball. Everything else is like a normal explosion: open stance, quick wrist cock, then hit down harder than usual, since you have to move more sand than if the ball were sitting cleanly on top. Be sure to follow through; simply punching the clubhead down behind the ball and leaving it there might move the ball, but probably not enough to get it out of the trap. This is not a shot you can spin, since the lie forces you to take a lot of sand; nor is it a shot you should expect to get close, although practice will increase your feel for the shot.

Buried Lie

If you find your ball mostly covered by sand, you've got your work cut out for you. (Sometimes a ball will bury completely. When you think you've found it, you're allowed to brush away just enough sand to determine that it is a ball. If you play it out and discover that it wasn't your ball, there is no penalty.) Play the shot with a sand wedge, this time closing the face quite a bit at address and taking a very firm grip. On the downswing, concentrate on knifing the blade down *hard* about an inch behind the ball. The idea is to jar the ball free, and that takes a lot of force—I've seen very few people explode too far from a buried lie, but I've watched plenty leave this shot in the bunker. And, believe me, just getting out and on the green is "mission accomplished"!

Close the clubface slightly to dig the ball out of a buried lie.

If the lie is downhill, make sure your knees, hips, and shoulders are parallel to the angle of the slope and play the ball a little farther back in your stance than usual.

Sloping Lies

Most bunkers aren't completely flat-bottomed, so occasionally you're going to face a sloping lie. Of the two—downhill and uphill—downhill is definitely the tougher.

The danger when playing from a downhill lie in sand is that the flange will skip off the slanted surface and you'll belly the ball. To prevent that, play the ball back a little farther than normal at address. Set up and swing as you would from a flat lie, making sure that the lines of your knees, hips, and shoulders are parallel to the angle of the slope—don't compensate by flexing your right knee too much.

Uphill lies don't pose much of a problem. The direction of the

From an uphill lie, again make sure that your body lines are parallel to the slope, and play the ball slightly farther forward.

slope will naturally force more weight onto your right foot, but don't worry about that. Simply make sure that your body lines are parallel to the slope, and let the weight fall where it will. Play the shot as a normal explosion, making sure to hit a little harder than from a flat lie, because the upward angle of the slope will cause the shot to fly higher and land softer.

Over a Steep Face

Here's a tough shot made easy. Picture your ball in a very deep bunker or close to the front lip. The only way to get it out and onto the green is with an extremely fast-rising explosion. To do that, hold the club loosely and let the blade fall open extremely wide; then turn your hands into a weak grip position. Set up for a typical explosion and release the club down briskly an inch behind; the ball will float out high and land soft. Claude Harmon, 1948 Masters champion, developed this technique for the deep bunkers of Winged Foot, in Mamaroneck, New York, and it's come in handy on some courses we see on tour, since many of them feature deep, steep-faced bunkers.

To hit an ultrahigh explosion—say, if your lie is close to the front lip—turn the blade wide open . . .

. . . make a good, long swing . . .

. . . and hit down *hard* an inch behind the ball,

In order to beat the back lip, you first have to get a stable stance, especially if you're forced to stand with your right foot out of the trap.

Beating the Back Lip

If your ball comes to rest close to the back lip, you've got a problem, since you won't have much room to slide the club under the ball. Instead, you'll have to swing the club back and down on a very steep angle. If there isn't much room behind the ball—say, less than six inches—I'll play out laterally instead of risking a mishit (unless it's match play and my opponent is in a position leaving me nothing to lose). If you elect to play to the pin, first get into a stable address

Pick the club up as abruptly as you can with a sharp wrist cock . . .

position, which may take a second to establish since one foot will be in the sand, one foot out. Open the clubface slightly, and then pick the clubhead up as abruptly as you can and hit straight down behind the ball. Of course, you won't be able to be precise with this shot; just getting it on the green is good work.

. . . and hit straight down behind the ball. Just getting this shot on the green is good work.

Chipping from Sand

You may run into a green-side sand situation in which it's actually a better play to chip the ball cleanly off the surface. For example, if there's little or no lip to negotiate and the pin is on the far side of the green, allowing plenty of space to work with, I may decide to play a chip and run with a middle iron instead of a long explosion. The final (and most important) requirement for chipping is that the lie must be clean and preferably flat. Conditions have to be perfect before I'll try this shot because it allows little margin for error. As mentioned earlier in this chapter, if you plan to pick the ball cleanly but accidentally get a little sand before hitting the ball, that sand will deaden the club-to-ball contact, usually enough to keep the ball from getting out of the trap. If you don't happen to strike the ball flush, it's better to hit it thin than fat in this case, because the shot will at least make it out of the hazard.

If everything is in favor of playing a chip, here's how to do it. First, stance should be the same as for a normal chip, but make sure to dig your feet in enough to form a solid base, since you can't risk any kind of upper-body motion or sway. (Remember to choke down a bit to make up for digging your feet in.) Play the ball back a little farther than you would for a normal chip, opposite center, to improve the chances of hitting the ball first. Zero in on the back of the ball and work hard on keeping a steady head and making crisp, clean contact. Again, use your arms and hands the same way you would on a normal chip shot.

Wet Sand

When sand is wet, the grains cling together, making the surface firmer than when dry. Due to this, the flange of a normal sand wedge is likely to bounce directly off the top of the sand and into the ball, instead of digging under before bouncing through. So from wet sand, you'll be better off playing the shot as a normal explosion, but with a pitching wedge. The sharper face and smaller flange are more conducive for slicing into the mudlike conditions.

> **The most important requirement for chipping is that the lie must be clean and preferably flat.**

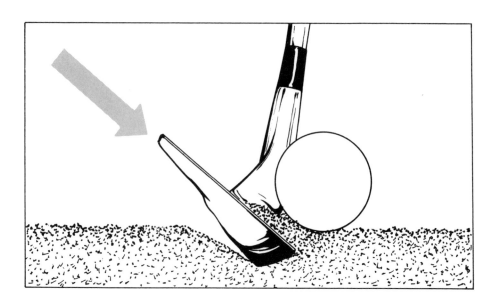

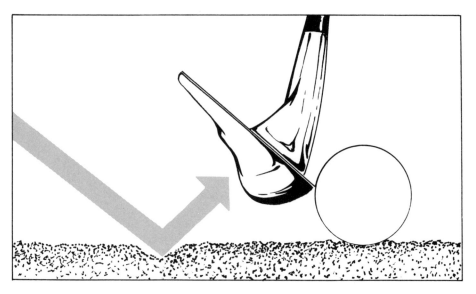

A sand wedge is liable to bounce off the surface of wet sand, resulting in a bladed shot. Instead, use the sharper-edged pitching wedge to cut underneath the ball.

9
GETTING UP AND DOWN

Whenever I play in a pro-am and one of my partners misses a green with his or her approach, I know it's a pretty safe bet that he or she will end up with bogey instead of saving par. I'd guess that chipping and pitching are the most neglected parts of the recreational player's game. If (and when) the typical amateur finds time to practice, it usually means hitting balls on the driving range for a little while, then maybe going to the practice green to stroke some putts. For many, the only chips and pitches they ever hit are those they face on the course.

Players who do find the time to practice a fair amount usually spend most of it hitting full shots in an effort to lower their handicaps, although the best way to knock off up to five or six strokes lies in improving a shoddy short game. When you play for a living, making a good salary means making a lot of birdies. Mere survival, on the other hand, depends on saving par when you miss a green—you aren't going to last too long if you can't manage to get up and down most of the time. Even the pros have days when their ball-striking isn't quite up to snuff, then end up missing a number of greens in the course of 18 holes. Those are the days when you have to rely on good chipping and pitching (and putting) to scratch out a decent score. But don't get the idea that you can live constantly on your short game. As Lee Trevino once said, there are two things that won't last: dogs that chase cars and pros who putt for pars!

Good pitching and chipping will also help you keep a good round alive. Even on a good ball-striking day, few players are going to hit 18 out of 18 greens, and it's bad news to blemish a good card with bogeys when greens are missed. The shots saved around the greens are what keep a great round going.

A good short game can also have a positive effect on your long game, as an old college buddy proved to me. This guy went to school

Over the road and onto the green: hitting my approach on the 16th hole during the fourth round of the '88 U.S. Open.

to play football but really liked golf, though he was pretty erratic; his long game wasn't too accurate, and he was a basket case when it came to short shots. He wasn't one to practice much, so his game always stayed at that level, until one fall after I'd finished my competitive schedule and had gone back home to kick my feet up for a while and we went out for a casual round. Not only did this guy hit a slew of greens, but he chipped and pitched the ball close enough to sink the putt most of the time when he didn't. Afterward, when we were sipping beers in the grill room and his score had been added for a 74, I asked him when he'd found the time to overhaul his whole game (since school he'd become a successful lawyer and kept a busy schedule). After all, it was all he could do to break 85 in the past.

"No overhaul," he answered. "I just spent a little practice time on improving my short game. The funny thing about it was that as my confidence got better at getting down in two from off the green, I stopped worrying so much about hitting a bad approach shot. When I stopped worrying about that, I stopped steering the ball and found myself making a bolder, more aggressive swing, and as a result, I started hitting my shots a lot more solid and straight."

That should be some food for thought. . . .

CHIPPING

I like to think of a chip as being nothing more than an extension of a putt, so I always want to get the ball down and rolling on the surface as soon as possible, which means landing it on the green close to the edge. Club selection depends on how far from the edge the ball

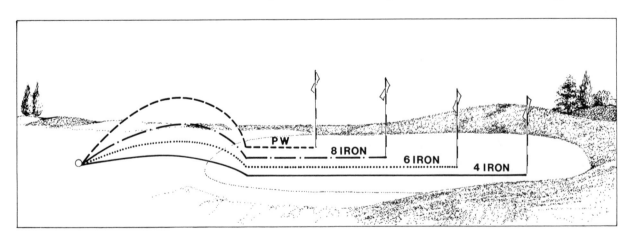

My chipping strategy is to get the ball onto the green as quickly as possible and let it roll to the hole. Club selection should depend on how far from the edge of the green the ball is, as well as how far the pin is from the edge.

lies and how far from the edge the flag is, because the object is to land the ball on the surface just past the fringe, then to let it roll to the hole on its own momentum.

For example, if my ball were five feet from the edge and the pin were 12 feet from the edge, I'd take a wedge and loft it just past the fringe—from there it should stop within three feet of the cup. Given the same lie with the pin 25 feet from the edge, I'd take a 7- or 8-iron (which will fly lower and thus roll farther than a wedge) and do the same thing: loft the ball just over the fringe on the proper line—and let it roll to the pin. This method was taught to me by Chandler Harper, who learned it from the great amateur Bobby Jones, so it must be pretty good advice.

When selecting which club to use, however, remember that you've got more than distance to contend with, since every green has slopes and contours that will affect the speed and direction of the shot. If the surface is naturally very slick or downhill, I'll want to use a more lofted club. I might, however, face a shot with the same distance to the edge and pin but a surface that slopes against me or is extremely slow; then I'd want less loft to give the shot more force. Notice that my object is always to change the loft of the club to determine how hard the shot is hit, while keeping the mechanics of the stroke the same every time. To get a feel for how far the ball carries and runs with each club, do some experimenting on the practice green. Don't be afraid to use a low-lofted club—Raymond Floyd, an excellent chipper, will use a 2-iron if he has little fringe to carry and a lot of green to work with.

What I like best about this strategy is that once you've decided what club to use and have aimed yourself in the direction you want to hit, you can forget about the pin and concentrate solely on carrying the ball just past the fringe and onto the green. As veteran pro Don January once told me, "When the pressure's on, get the ball on the ground as quick as you can." I've found this to be excellent advice.

Get the ball safely down and running when you have a lot of green to work with.

Mechanics of the Chipping Stroke

The mechanics of my chipping stroke are almost exactly the same as for my putting stroke, with two differences. The first is stance—compared with how I stand for putting, it's narrower and slightly open. That's how I do it; you can vary your address position as long as you're comfortable and balanced once over the ball.

The second difference is that I don't want to keep the clubhead quite so low to the ground on the backswing; instead, it moves back on a slightly sharper angle, so the ball can be struck with a more

I prefer a narrow, slightly open chipping stance—the ball opposite my right heel. I hold the club with the same grip that I use for putting—reverse overlap—and choke down for added control.

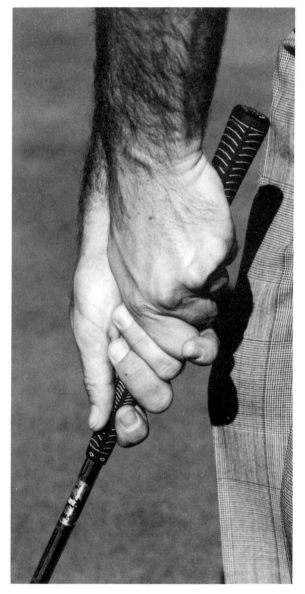

The mechanics of the swing are very similar to the putting stroke, except I want to move the club back and through on a sharper angle to ensure making a slightly descending blow.

descending blow. (The backswing should still start smoothly, and the overall motion should be rhythmic, as when putting.) Everything else is virtually the same: hands over the ball at address and the stroke mainly an arm-and-shoulder motion, keeping the triangle intact, with a slight cocking and uncocking of the wrists. I always choke down to the end of the grip for maximum clubhead control and use the same grip—reverse overlap—I use to putt with, holding on firmly with the last three fingers of my left hand.

Concentrate on keeping your hands slightly ahead of the clubhead through impact and keeping the clubhead moving toward the target.

Chip Tips

The chip is a fairly simple motion, but it demands concentration because anything short of crisp contact is going to reduce greatly the chances of putting the ball close. Following are a few tips that should help you get better results.

At address, set most of your weight on your left side, which helps make a descending blow. Bear in mind that the chip is a precision shot that should be caressed, not hit hard, so be sure not to squeeze the club too tightly or push the clubhead down in the grass so that it catches on the takeaway.

To avoid mishits, keep your head from swiveling toward the target until after the ball is gone. Note that my lower body has stayed in the same position as it was upon impact—only my arms and shoulders have moved.

I like to concentrate on swinging the club straight back and straight through toward my landing point, keeping my hands even with the ball through impact and the clubface square to the target line on the follow-through, just like when putting. The combination of a square clubface moving straight along the target line produces a shot that lands with a little backspin (which should be killed on the first bounce) and rolls straight. Poor clubhead path and/or clubface alignment at impact will result either in pushing or pulling the ball off line or in imparting sidespin that will make the chip bounce left or right.

Chipping Strategy

I've always looked at chipping as an offensive part of the game—it's a shot I think about making, not just getting close. I don't extensively read it as I do a putt, but I do take a few seconds to determine which way it will break, if any. As when putting, ideally I want the speed of the ball to carry it only a few inches past if I miss, since it wouldn't be smart to "go for it" and leave a five-footer to finish. Of course, it isn't realistic to sink certain chips, just as you don't really expect to sink certain putts. If a chip shot is exceptionally long or there's a lot of break, I'll be very happy to get down in two and head to the next tee.

PITCHING

When does a shot change from being a long chip to a pitch? In my book, when the distance you have to hit the ball is so long that it requires extra wrist cock, which you can't get by using the reverse overlap grip, the shot officially changes from a chip to a pitch. Pitching is a little more difficult than chipping since it's a longer shot, requiring a longer swing, so you shouldn't expect to put the ball as close consistently, though that is your ultimate goal. Although a pitch is longer than a chip, you should still think of it in terms of precision, not power.

A pitch is a lofted shot, usually played with a wedge, that carries most of the way to the target. To get it close, you have to be accurate in both direction and distance, and the better you are at pinpointing both, the more strokes you'll save.

> **Although a pitch is longer than a chip, you should still think of it in terms of precision, not power.**

Pitching Mechanics

Because a pitch is longer than a chip, it requires more clubhead speed to loft the ball to the target than can be comfortably generated by just the hands, wrists, and shoulders. You've got to incorporate some of the power of the big muscles and concentrate on keeping intact the triangle formed by your arms and shoulders.

Set up in a narrow (feet just inside shoulder width), open stance, with the ball just forward of center. You should feel comfortable, with your body in a compact, but not cramped, position. You should also be relaxed, especially your forearms and hands: *pitching requires feel and finesse, which tension destroys.* To relieve tension, take a couple of practice swings.

The key to getting the big muscles of the back and legs into the act here is to concentrate on shifting the triangle on the backswing and downswing. On the downswing, keep the right shoulder from dropping; dropsliding on a pitch shot will result in hitting behind the ball and dumping it short. Usually dropsliding is the result of trying to scoop, or lift, the ball into the air. Instead, hit down and the ball will go up.

Sand Wedge vs. Pitching Wedge

The sand wedge isn't used just for getting out of bunkers; it's also an excellent club to pitch with, especially for very lofted shots. It has more loft than a pitching wedge, and the large flange will slide through light rough easier than a sharper-faced pitching wedge. Avoid the SW, however, if the lie is hard and tight, since the round flange can easily bounce off the surface and into the ball, resulting in a bladed shot.

Less-than-Full Wedges

I hit a full pitching wedge 118 yards; a full sand wedge, 90 yards. Hitting the ball shorter than that requires a less-than-full swing—which can be tricky as far as getting the proper distance is concerned. There are several methods for doing this.

First, you can gauge the length of your backswing to determine how far the ball goes. For example, find out how far you hit it when you swing your left arm back into the 9 o'clock position, then the 10 o'clock and 11 o'clock positions. Then, after determining the length of shot you need to hit, figure how far back to swing your left arm and execute.

Another way to regulate distance is to choke down on the grip; how far depends on the length of shot needed. The farther you move your hands down on the grip, the shorter the shot will fly. That's because by choking down you're shortening the effective length of the shaft, which shrinks the size of the swing arc and automatically helps limit the length of your backswing, both of which reduce clubhead speed.

However you decide to regulate distance, don't forsake feel for a totally mechanical approach. In fact, once you gain feel, which comes through practice, you won't have to think so much in terms of mechanical thoughts like length of backswing or how far to choke down; the force of the swing will come naturally. It will become just like putting. When you step up to a 40-footer, do you consciously think of how far back you want to swing the putterhead? I doubt it.

For a pitch shot, choke down and set up open, with the ball just forward of center.

Swing the club back by shifting your weight, coiling the large upper-body muscles, and cocking your wrists.

Concentrate on keeping your right shoulder from dropping through impact, and keep the clubface pointing skyward in the follow-through.

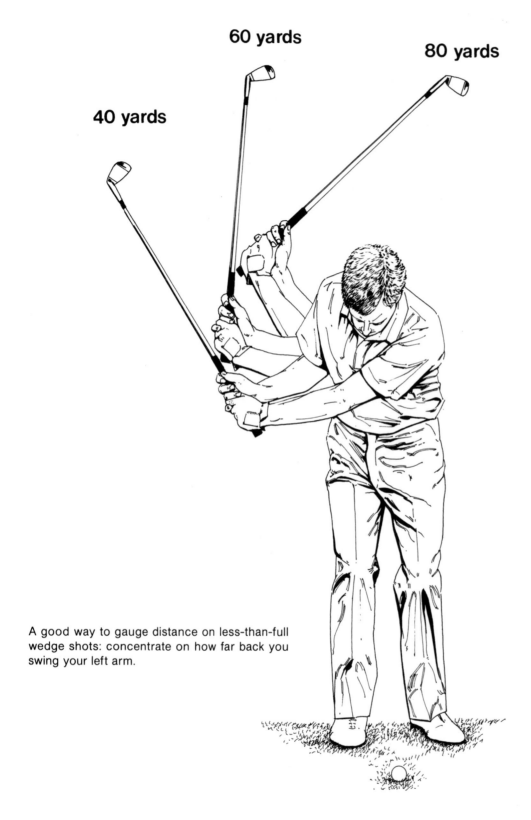

40 yards

60 yards

80 yards

A good way to gauge distance on less-than-full wedge shots: concentrate on how far back you swing your left arm.

You stroke the ball as hard as feel tells you to, which is the same way you'll start approaching long and short pitch shots if you hit enough of them. So next time you hit a few practice putts before a round, give some thought to hitting a few practice pitches, too. I always like to end my practice sessions by hitting at least four or five wedges of different lengths, as well.

Above all, don't overcomplicate these kinds of shots. The swing is simply a miniature version of the full swing, so remember always to shift center and to release the club with your hands, since there's a tendency on a shorter swing to hold on through impact.

Pressure Pitching

Because these shots require extensive use of the smaller muscles, they're going to be more difficult to hit under pressure than a full-swing shot. In 1986 I was in a sudden-death playoff with Calvin Peete at the Houston Open. On the first play-off hole, I missed the green to the right and faced a pitch of about 25 yards. Calvin was on the green about 15 feet from the flag, so I figured I'd have to get up and down from where I was to at least salvage a tie on the hole. As I made my practice swings, my key thoughts were to stay completely relaxed from my shoulders down, so my arms felt very fluid, and to concentrate on keeping my grip light enough so I could feel the weight of the clubhead throughout the motion and let it do the work. I stepped up to the ball, stayed loose, and swung the clubhead back and through, letting it accelerate down the way a string of cars on a roller coaster builds speed through a large dip. The ball rose nicely, arched, and dropped just short of the pin, stopping three feet away. Calvin lagged his close and tapped in; I sank mine, then won with a birdie on the third play-off hole.

The Cut-Lob

The cut-lob is a variation of the basic pitch shot that rises on a steeper trajectory, flies higher, and drops dead. It's the shot you need when there's a bunker between your ball and the green, and the pin is cut close to the sand, giving you little green to work with.

To play the shot, open your stance a little more than you would for a normal pitch and open the clubface to increase the effective loft, aiming it slightly left of your target. Cock your wrists quickly on the backswing; then hit down briskly, making a conscious effort to let the clubhead pass your hands and slide under the ball at impact instead

Above all, don't try to overcomplicate these kinds of shots.

The cut-lob flies high and drops dead. To play it, open your stance a little more than for a normal pitch and lay the clubface wide open.

Pick the club up quickly with the small muscles of the hands and wrists . . .

. . . and try to slice the blade cleanly under the ball, keeping the clubface open through impact, and letting the clubhead pass your hands.

The ball will pop almost straight up.

of rolling your right wrist over your left. The more you open your stance and clubface, the higher and shorter the shot will go.

When deciding whether to play the cut-lob, make sure the lie is favorable, because it's a low-percentage shot. A soft, cushiony lie makes it easiest to slide the clubface under the ball, which is why this is a good shot to play from light rough. You can try it if the lie is tight, but there's practically no margin for error, and mishitting a cut-lob can be deadly—you'll end up either blading it over the green or hitting it fat and short.

When you make the downswing, make sure to accelerate. Too many weekend players chicken out on this shot on the downswing and make a tentative pass at it, resulting in a weak or mishit shot.

The Bump-and-Run

Another variation of the pitch is the bump-and-run shot, a low shot that bounces sooner and rolls more to get to its destination. In the past, when courses were harder, the bump-and-run was used a lot more, but today's softer conditions make it more favorable to loft most shots to the hole from 20 to 80 yards away. Still, you'll sometimes face circumstances that warrant playing the shot low and "bumping" it to the flag. The setup and mechanics for this shot are the same as with a chip, and feel is all-important. The loft of the club should depend on how low you want to hit it, but it will usually be somewhere between a 5- and an 8-iron.

If I'm hitting to a two-tiered green and the pin is on the farther, upper tier, I'll usually bump it onto the lower level and let it roll to the hole. Make sure when doing this, though, that the ball is down and rolling before it gets to the upslope. If it's still bouncing, it could bounce directly into the hill, killing the shot; or it could take a big bounce completely over the slope and roll over the back of the green.

Another time I might bump the ball is when my ball lies at the bottom of a banked side of a green and the pin is close to that side, giving me little surface area to work with. I can either play a delicate cut-lob and try to land the ball precisely in the area between the pin and the green's edge or bump it firmly into the hill so that it jumps up over the top and rolls to the flag.

"THIRD" WEDGE

Another equipment innovation of the 1980s is a utility club known as the "third" wedge, which boasts 60 degrees of loft, as compared to the standard pitching wedge (approximately 52 degrees) and sand wedge (approximately 56 degrees). Though it's possible to add extra loft to your sand or pitching wedge by opening the clubface, doing so also adds bounce to the flange, making it tough to play from a tight lie. The third wedge, which has a sharp leading edge and no bounce on the bottom, allows you to play a very high lob with a square clubface from just about any kind of lie. Though I don't use one, many tour players have opted to remove a club from their bag to make room for a third wedge as an extra weapon around the greens.

Examine the conditions to see if they're conducive to playing the pitch low and "bumping" it toward the pin.

It helps to have a good imagination to play this kind of shot, because the better you can visualize where to bounce it into the slope and how hard to hit it, the better your chances of pulling it off. As with the cut-lob, once you've decided to play this type of shot, don't get tentative. Decelerating on the downswing will result in a weak attempt that dies on the hill and may roll back down to your feet. You at least want to get the ball somewhere on the green.

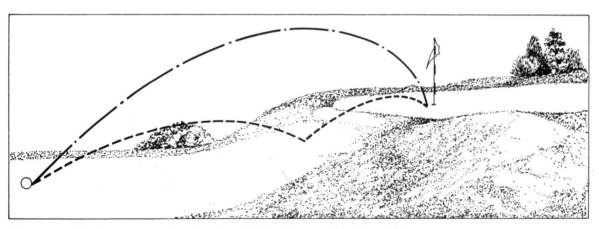

Always consider two ways to play the shot—high or low—and decide which is best.

10
PRACTICE, PRACTICE, PRACTICE

It's time to talk about a subject that isn't exactly near and dear to the hearts of most amateurs, and that's practice. Most people look at it as if it were liver—although they know it's good for them, they don't like it, and so they avoid it.

I'm not going to tell you that you have to practice, because if your attitude is negative in the first place, you won't get much out of it anyway. I'd just like to talk about the benefits of practice; also, I'll tell you how I approach it, what I feel it does for me, and how you can use your practice time wisely.

MOVEMENT MEMORY

Why does a baseball player take batting practice? To stay familiar with the movement of his swing, so that when he steps up to the plate he doesn't have to think mechanically about his footwork or bat position; he's become so familiar with it through practice that he can devote his full concentration on reacting to the pitch. Swinging the

1987 Ryder Cup at Muirfield Village: Captain Jack Nicklaus (center) gives advice during a practice round to (left to right) me, Larry Mize, Scott Simpson, and Tom Kite.

bat has become second nature to him; he can do it without consciously thinking about his physical movements.

All of us have done one thing or another so often that we can do it without thinking about it. Take driving a car; when you first started learning, your mind was consumed with the feeling of the steering wheel in your hands, staying in your lane, bringing the vehicle to a smooth stop, and so forth. But through practice, driving became second nature, and you're able to think of other things as you cruise along.

That's part of the overall benefit of going to the practice range: becoming familiar enough with the swing so you don't have to think consciously about every move you're making, but instead have it happen automatically. That's not just for tee-to-green shots, but also

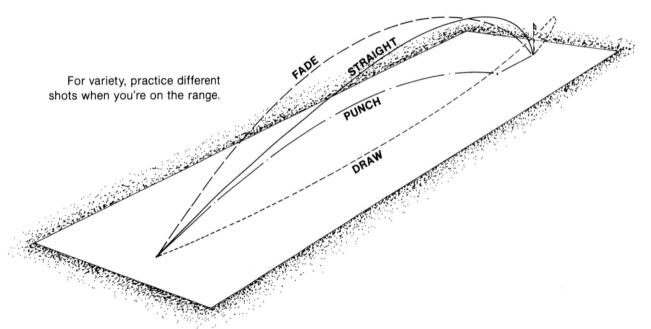

For variety, practice different shots when you're on the range.

for pitches, chips, and putts. A popular term in sports is "muscle memory," which refers to the body's ability to memorize how a motion feels and thus repeat it. I like to think about it as "movement memory," since that's what golf is: moving your body properly so that you can move the club properly, so that you can move the ball properly.

If the only movement memory you ever practice is on the golf course, you're cheating yourself. On the course you have to wait a few minutes between hitting shots and mix full swings with short shots and putts. But by hitting a lot of shots in succession on the practice tee or a lot of chips in succession on the practice green, you become familiar with the motion much more quickly.

FIXING A FAULT

If you've developed a swing fault (and we all do from time to time), the practice ground is the least frustrating place to work on fixing it, as opposed to trying to find the cure on the course. The reason is obvious: in practice, you can experiment without having to pay the penalty for a poor result, be it an errant shot or a bad putt, whereas trying to fix something during a round can lead to a worse shot, which leads to more frustration. If a chink finds its way into any part of your game, the fastest and least aggravating way to work it out is off the course.

Be patient when trying to work out a problem. Occasionally you'll see immediate improvement, but don't become disillusioned with practice if you don't. Most faults don't happen overnight, but gradually, so you can't always expect the cure to happen instantaneously—it may take a matter of days, or even weeks. For example, an amateur friend of mine had the habit of lifting his left heel way up off the ground on his backswing. It wasn't a terrible fault, but I knew that he'd be more stable at the top if he didn't pick the heel up so far, so I recommended that he work on not lifting it so high. Although it sounds like a simple adjustment, it took my friend about two weeks of practice before he could keep his heel down without having to think about it.

Be patient when trying to work out a problem. Don't become disillusioned with practice if you don't see immediate improvement.

PREVENTIVE MEDICINE

Most pros look at the driving range as a place to practice preventive medicine; it's where they can stop swing faults from happening before they start. For example, I check my alignment at least once a week by laying two clubs down on the ground, parallel to each other—one just outside my toes, the other just outside the ball. Using them as reference, I can check my body alignment to make sure I haven't slipped into an open or closed position without realizing it, and I check the direction of my divots, making sure they point slightly inside my target line. This exercise is simple and invaluable, but it's not allowed on the golf course—only during practice.

Two other things I always make a point of monitoring during practice at least once a week are grip position and weight shift. When I play my best golf, the *V*s of both hands point at my right eye, so I want to make sure they don't stray. In regard to weight shift, I want to be sure I'm getting behind the ball and fully on the inside of my right foot at the top of my swing with every club from driver through short irons.

A common sight on any professional practice tee is a pro using two clubs to check body alignment, clubface alignment, and divot direction.

Notice that all the elements I've listed here—alignment, divot direction (swing path), grip position, and weight shift—are fundamentals. The fact that I check mine frequently should demonstrate to you how important they are and how easy it can be to slip away from them and into bad habits.

INTELLIGENT PRACTICE MAKES PERFECT

Some people get more out of 20 minutes of practice than others get from an hour, because they know how to practice intelligently. Here are a few tips on how to get the most out of your practice time.

Don't Just Beat Balls

Your mind should be at work as much as your body is when you practice. Whenever I hit a range ball I'm always conscious of how the shot should have behaved, be it a draw or fade. I'm usually thinking about some aspect of my swing, be it weight shift, hand position, rhythm, or tempo. I don't mean to imply that you should be grinding intensely on every shot, but to get the most out of it, you should have your mind on what you're doing.

Work on What Needs Work

Everybody has some part of his or her game that stands out above the rest. Say you're a pretty good driver—you enjoy hitting tee shots and you consider it your strong point. So it's not going to make a lot of sense to spend most of your practice time hitting drivers, even though it's fun. Common sense tells you that you'll benefit more from devoting most of your practice time to the things you *aren't* good at, even though it may be less enjoyable. If you're the type of person who likes a challenge, you'll find that tackling an area that needs improvement can be satisfying when performance starts to get better.

Always Hit to a Target

Golf is a target game: you aim for the fairway; then you aim for the green; then you aim for the cup. Yet all too often amateurs hit ball after ball off the practice tee without aiming at anything specific. It's easy to fool yourself into thinking your shots are going straight when hitting onto a range that's 100 yards wide, but you may find that you actually weren't that accurate when you tee it up on the course where boundaries are tight and you have to play the ball out of the hazards you hit into. *Always* aim at a target, even if you have to pick out a tree in the distance as an imaginary flag or two trees as boundaries of an imaginary fairway. For half and three-quarter wedge shots, pick out a specific spot against which to measure distance accuracy.

Avoiding Fatigue

The point of practice is to break bad habits and reinforce good ones, and the best circumstances in which to do this are when you're fresh and strong both mentally and physically. Whenever I reach a point when my head isn't in the game anymore or my muscles are tired out, I quit, because I know that I'm not going to get anything further out of forcing myself to continue.

If you aren't used to practicing, you'll probably get tired fairly quickly on the practice tee, since on the course you get to rest between shots. However, the more you practice, the more endurance you'll build up, and that strength should be reflected in a better performance when you play, especially toward the end of a round.

Stick with the Club Until You're Satisfied

It's best to start with the higher-lofted clubs first, because they require shorter swings. Then work your way up through the bag as your muscles loosen up. One suggestion I'd like to make is to stick with whatever club you're using until you're hitting it decently. If you start out pulling your wedge shots to the left, switching to a 9-iron isn't going to make the problem go away. The trouble isn't the club but some element of the swing, so stay with whatever you're using until you've at least made some improvement. Otherwise, the trouble will simply spread to the next club, and then the next.

Psychological Pluses

I mentioned that practice helps you become physically familiar with the motions needed to produce certain types of shots. It also provides you with a psychological familiarity that will help on the course, especially when you're playing under pressure. For example, suppose you're playing a match and your opponent is safely on the green, while you're faced with a difficult pitch over a bunker to a tight pin. Knowing that you spent some time practicing cut-lob shots for a couple of days beforehand is going to supply a self-confidence that will help make the shot happen. Or it might be a four-foot putt that you need to sink on the last hole to tie the match. Knowing that you sank 25 four-footers in a row on the practice green the night before is going to help put you in the right frame of mind to hole that putt.

Probably the best story I can think of from my own experience that illustrates the way practice can cushion your performance under pressure comes from the 1988 U.S. Open. On the fourth day I came

> **The point of practice is to break bad habits and reinforce good ones.**

to the final tee, tied with Nick Faldo. Both of us drove in the fairway, but Nick put his approach 30 feet from the pin, while I bunkered mine. Needless to say, I knew I had to get up and down, since I doubted Nick was going to three-putt from where he was. My lie was clean and slightly uphill—it really wasn't a difficult shot, but under those circumstances any shot is hard. As I dug my feet in and settled over the ball, I kept reminding myself that I knew this shot, that I'd practiced it a thousand times before. Then I made a confident swing that put the ball three feet from the hole. Faldo barely missed his birdie and tapped in. Then I sank my par putt to force a play-off.

HOW I PRACTICE
Preround Warm-Up

I hit practice balls before every round, more as a warm-up than to work on swing mechanics. I always loosen up with these irons:

Club	Number of balls
PW	10-12
7-iron	7-8
5-iron	7-8
3-iron	7-8
4-wood	2-3
3-wood	2-3
Driver	5-7

If you add up the numbers you'll find that I'll hit roughly 40 to 50 shots before a round (a little more than the average pro), which gives me the feeling that I've already done some playing when I get to the first tee, which is how I want to feel.

After I'm finished on the range I head for the practice green and hit putts for about 15 minutes before teeing off. Again, before a round I'm not thinking in terms of putting mechanics; instead, I am just trying to get a feel for the speed of the greens.

I think that amateurs often waste strokes in the first couple of holes of a round because they don't warm up first. It takes a couple of holes to get loose. If you can, get to the course a little early so you can hit a few balls before teeing off—the time will be well spent. If you can't hit some warm-up shots, I recommend loosening up by swinging a weighted club or a couple of long irons. Start slow, with half-swings, gradually lengthening to full ones. Next, take a few minutes to hit some pitches and chips, concentrating on smooth

Amateurs waste strokes because they don't warm up first. It takes a couple of holes to get loose.

rhythm and solid contact. Finally, stroke some putts from different distances to get a feel for the speed of the greens. The average time for your warm-up should be 20 to 30 minutes.

Postround Practice

I always go to the practice range after playing (unless weather or darkness doesn't allow it) to work with the clubs I skipped during warm-up—the 9-, 8-, 6-, 4-, and 2-irons. If I've been playing well I usually hit a bucket of balls, then quit and go back to the practice green to hit pitches, chips, sand shots, and putts. However, if I think there's a mechanical problem that's developed in my swing, I'll usually stay until I've worked it out. There are few times during a season when my swing feels perfect, and when that happens I'll hit very few balls and work mostly on putting instead. Often I'll key on

Nobody practices the short game—pitching, chipping, and putting—enough!

slowing down my rhythm and tempo if I feel that they quickened during the course of 18 holes.

Okay, you may be reading this, thinking, *That's fine for Curtis Strange to spend that much time practicing, but I can't afford to.* I certainly understand, and I don't expect you to invest the same amount of time practicing your game that a professional player does. I just want to impress upon you that practice is an important contibutor to being a good player—I wouldn't spend so much time doing it if it didn't help and I didn't enjoy it. If you use your head, practice, even a little, will benefit your game—it certainly can't hurt, and it can be fun.

GETTING FROM THE PRACTICE TEE TO THE COURSE

A common complaint about practice that I've heard from my pro-am partners is that after hitting the ball well on the range, they come out and play like dogs on the course. What's the reason? Score. When you're on the range, there's no pressure to score well—a poor shot is easily forgotten as you quickly tee up another. There's more psychological freedom on the practice tee; unfortunately, the pressure of scoring forces people into worrying too much about results instead of hitting the ball solidly, which forces them into steering the ball instead of letting go and putting a good swing on it. If you start worrying less about score, you'll start hitting the ball more like you do on the practice ground.

ONE CLUB
One Club is a practice game, the title of which is self-explanatory: you choose one club and play from tee to green (including holing out) using only that club. Though it might sound silly, it's actually a lot of fun, especially if you compete with a friend or two. Besides having fun, you'll also learn a lot about shotmaking when you find yourself with 100 yards to the green and a 4-iron in your hands, or if you have to blast out of a bunker with a 5-iron.

11
ARE GOLFERS ATHLETES?

If you've been playing golf for a minimum of a few years, I'll bet you've heard at least one friend snidely remark that "golfers aren't athletes" or that "golf isn't a *real* sport." I think the best response to these statements comes from Dr. Frank Jobe, the cofounder and executive medical director of the Centinela Hospital's Fitness Institute in Inglewood, California, and orthopedic consultant to the PGA Tour. In the introduction of the book *30 Exercises for Better Golf* (Inglewood: Champ Press, 1986), which he coauthored with Diane R. Moynes, Dr. Jobe had this to say:

> People often ask, "Are golfers really athletes?" "Yes," I tell them, no question about it, for golf is a sport and to play it well one must have athletic ability: strength, agility, coordination, and endurance. Unfortunately, the prototype golfer in the public's mind has long been the out-of-shape executive who rides a cart, plays 18 holes, and then retires to the 19th hole. Even at the professional level, golf has seldom been regarded as a sport that required vigorous or specific body conditioning, especially when even potbellied players were winning major tournaments. The prevailing attitude was that walking 18 holes and spending time on the driving range were enough to keep the "golfing muscles" in shape.
>
> These perceptions about golf are now changing, reflecting a growing awareness by amateurs and pros alike that a specific program of stretching and strengthening exercises will not only lower the risk of injury, but will improve performance—at every level of the game.

"... golf is a sport and to play it well one must have athletic ability: strength, agility, coordination, and endurance."
—Dr. Frank Jobe

Now, I couldn't have said all that better myself! I'm no expert, but it's always been my contention that tour pros were more athletically inclined than most average people. I think you could take any nine pros and stick us on a softball field and you'd have a pretty fair team. And I dare anyone who's ever seen Sam Snead strike a golf ball to tell me that that isn't an athletic movement. Sam's whole motion, from start to finish, is a magnificent combination of rhythm, power, and grace. There isn't a player on tour, men's or women's, who doesn't have excellent hand-to-eye coordination. Most have actively participated in other sports on a scholastic level and some beyond. Hale Irwin was an all-Big Eight defensive back at Colorado State. Tom Watson was a star quarterback in high school. Jack Nicklaus was a stand-out basketball player in high school. Raymond Floyd was offered a contract to pitch baseball professionally, while J. C. Snead actually did play a couple of years in the minor leagues. And how about Larry Nelson, another fine amateur baseball player who didn't actually start playing golf until he was 21, at which time he returned to the United States after serving in the Vietnam War.

I admit there are few golfers who are going to run the four-minute mile (all right, there are none who will), but you have to be in better shape than you think to compete on tour. The constant travel alone is wearing both physically and mentally, never mind the grind of walking a golf course six times a week, which is more work than some people think (especially those who have never done it). I'll never forget when Michael Jordan, basketball star for the Chicago Bulls and an avid golfer, told me that he felt more tired after playing a round of golf than he did after a basketball game, because in golf there's so much standing around, which to him is more taxing than running up and down a basketball court for 48 minutes.

I know for a fact that I'm in better shape now at age 34 than I've ever been, and I think a lot of my fellow competitors feel the same way. I can think of a few good reasons why I am. First is the influence of the general health-and-fitness craze that's taken place in America in the last 10 years or so. This trend has played a major role in raising the public's awareness about how exercising and eating right can help you feel better, function better, and live longer.

Second, every person who plays golf for a living knows that his or her body is the machine that swings the club, and the better he or she takes care of that machine, the better it's going to perform and the less likely it is to break down. In a golfer's case, the part that's most likely to give out is the back, so most players realize that it's smart to do anything they can to prevent injury.

Unfortunately, preventing injury also means limiting leisure-time activities if they pose a high risk. In other words, doing anything that might result in an injury that could hamper swinging a golf club is definitely out. Nobody got a bigger kick out of a pickup basketball game than I did until I broke the ring finger on my left hand while playing a couple of years ago. I haven't played since, now limiting my extracurricular athletic activity to jogging.

I recommend that amateurs become fit: if you feel better about yourself, that confidence will be reflected in a better performance.

However, I encourage amateurs, who don't count on their golf games to make a living, to be active in other sports. Any sport or exercise that increases your strength and endurance is going to be helpful to your golf game. Besides the physical benefits, the more competitive experience you get, the better you'll be able to sustain the winning edge. That goes for whether you're competing at something athletic, like tennis, or nonathletic, like checkers or bridge. My feeling has always been that whatever you're playing, you should play to win in the spirit of good sportsmanship. That way, if you lose, you have the satisfaction of knowing that you tried your best.

A final reason for staying in good physical shape is the psychological boost it provides. The competition on tour is so intense that almost anyone can win in a given week. So if a guy feels as if he's gaining an edge by exercising and taking care of himself, you can bet he'll do it. That's another reason I recommend that amateurs become fit: if you feel better about yourself, that confidence will be reflected in a better performance.

THE FITNESS CENTER

One of the best things to happen for us tour players, in my opinion, was when the Fitness Center came out on tour in 1975. Housed in a trailer, the Fitness Center is pulled by a tractor-trailer truck and travels to just about every tour site in the country. It's specially equipped with exercise equipment for the pros to use under the supervision of a physical therapist and two athletic trainers.

Not only can the players exercise at the trailer, but they can also get expert treatment for any aches, pains, and injuries that might result from playing. I have a history of throwing my back out of whack once in a while, and whenever it happens the first thing I try to do is head for the trailer to have it worked on. There are a lot of bad backs on tour; shoulder and wrist injuries are also fairly prevalent. Most players who have ailments take advantage of the Fitness Center and the people who work there, while many other players make use of it to prevent injury and improve performance by strengthening and conditioning the "golfing muscles."

The golfing muscles were identified by Dr. Jobe and a team of medical researchers at Centinela Hospital through the extensive study they conducted to arrive at the information published in the previously mentioned book *30 Exercises for Better Golf*. In it, they refute the old idea that the muscles in the hands and forearms are the most important, along with the legs, when it comes to swinging a golf club.

They determined that the leg muscles do indeed play an important role in the swing, but also that the big muscles of the upper body—chest (pectorals), back (*latissimus dorsi*), and small shoulder muscles (rotator cuffs)—were much bigger contributors to generating club-head speed than the muscles from the elbows down. Not that strengthening the hands, wrists, and forearms won't improve your club control; they simply discovered that the real power sources were the pecs, lats, and rotator cuffs. Therefore, any exercises that strengthen and increase the flexibility of these muscles will increase the efficiency of your swing and decrease your chances of injury.

EXERCISES FOR GOLFERS

Following are a few exercises that will enhance the performance of your golf muscles. Start out slowly, working with light weight and only two sets of 10 repetitions performed three times a week. After a few sessions, increase the weight and number of sets to three at 10 reps. Before starting any fitness program, however, Centinela recommends that you consult a physician. (Anyone interested in additional exercises that will add strength and flexibility to the golf muscles should consult *30 Exercises for Better Golf.*)

Building the chest muscles.

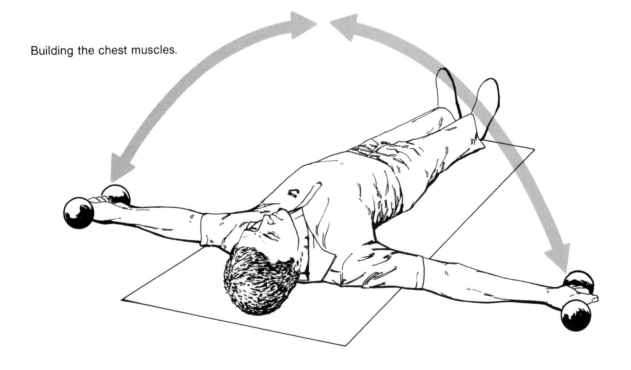

Chest

If you swing from the right side, the right pectoral muscle provides power, while the left helps keep the club under control as you swing down. An excellent way to strengthen the pecs is to lie on your back, arms straight out, palms facing up, with a weight in each hand. Keeping your elbows straight, lift your arms until they point to the ceiling; then lower them slowly.

Another way to strengthen the chest muscles is by doing some good, old-fashioned push-ups. Spread your hands to about shoulder width, with palms flat on the floor, even with the pecs. Keeping your back straight, lower your body until your nose is about an inch from the floor. If you aren't strong enough to do conventional push-ups, rest your knees on the ground and lift your body from the knees up.

Back

The large muscles in the back are called the *latissimus dorsi*. On the right-handed downswing, the left lat pulls, while the right helps stabilize the club through the follow-through. There are a number of ways to strengthen the lats, but some risk injury to the back, something golfers want to avoid as much as possible. The safest way is to do chin-ups, with your hands spread as wide apart as possible.

An alternative is to use a pull-down machine (most health clubs and gyms feature them), which allows you to sit down and pull weight downward. Pull-downs work the lat muscles the same way chin-ups do, but the machine allows you to regulate the amount of weight to less than your body weight, in case you aren't strong enough to do conventional chin-ups.

Legs

More specifically, I am referring to the big muscles in the thighs (called quadriceps), which are extremely important in adding stability to and generating power in the golf swing. If you're out of shape in this area, you'll begin to feel your legs getting tired toward the end of a round, and you'll unconsciously flex less at the knees to take the strain off them, changing your swing.

To strengthen the quadriceps, try wall squats: Lean your back against a wall, feet spread just inside shoulder width, heels about 12 inches from the base of the wall. Bend slowly at the knees, sliding your body downward, while keeping your back straight and flat against the wall. Lower yourself until you feel the tension in your thighs (approximately the level of a normal chair) and hold it for 10 seconds. As you get stronger, try holding the position for 20 seconds.

Strong quadriceps are crucial to a good golf game.

Shoulders

The large muscle in the shoulder, the deltoid, does not play a major role in the golf swing, but the rotator cuff (which is actually four small muscles underneath the deltoid) is an important stabilizer. There are three exercises to strengthen the specific parts of the rotator cuff that are important in the swing. To perform each, you'll need dumbbells, or else you can use surgical tubing as a form of resistance instead of dumbbells.

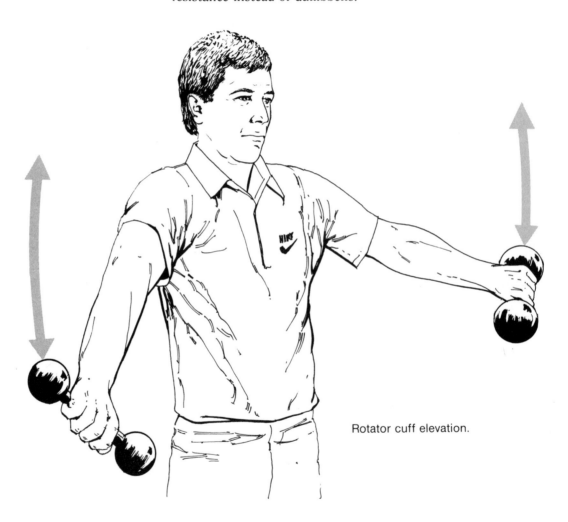

Rotator cuff elevation.

Rotator Cuff Elevation
Hold a weight in each hand, arms dangling at your sides, hands turned so your thumbs are toward the ground. Keeping your elbows straight, lift your arms upward, not straight out from your sides, but at an angle of about 30 degrees in front of you. Raise your arms to shoulder level, and then slowly lower them again.

Rotator cuff external rotation.

Rotator Cuff External Rotation

Lie on your side, supporting your head with one hand. Take a weight in the other hand, bending your elbow 90 degrees and holding it snugly against the side of your rib cage. Rest the weight on the floor and begin the repetition by lifting the weight until your arm points to the ceiling, keeping the elbow close to your side. Switch sides until you've done three sets with both arms.

Rotator Cuff Internal Rotation

Lie flat on your back, weight in the hand resting on the ground, arm bent 90 degrees, and elbow snugly to the side of the rib cage. Lift the weight smoothly until your arm points to the ceiling, and then lower it slowly back to the ground. Repeat with the other arm.

Rotator cuff internal rotation.

Stomach

The stomach, or abdominal, muscles don't particularly contribute to generating clubhead speed, but keeping them strong helps to relieve some of the strain that the normal golf swing imposes on the back. However, the sit-up, which most people know strengthens the abs, can actually result in back injury. A much safer way to strengthen the stomach muscles is by doing abdominal curls. Lie on your back, knees bent about 90 degrees, feet flat on the ground. Stretch your arms toward your feet, palms facing the floor, and lift your head and shoulders just off the floor, exhaling to a count of five before lowering them slowly back to the floor. This sounds easier than it looks—most people will have a hard time completing ten the first time. As you get stronger, increase to 20, then 30 curls. You can also vary it by crossing your arms across your chest or putting your hands behind your head.

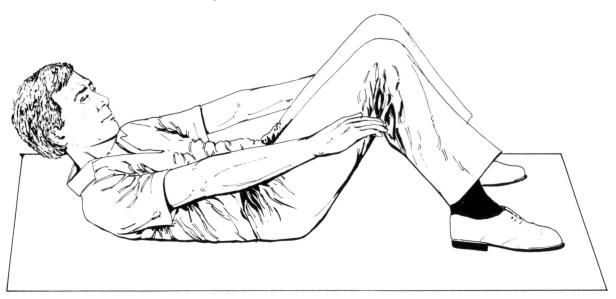

Building strength in the abdominal muscles will help relieve strain on the back.

GOLF IS A SPORT AND SHOULD BE APPROACHED AS ONE

I highly recommend exercising to increase your strength, improve your mental outlook, and prevent injury. But Dr. Jobe can say it better than I can:

> Golf is a sport and you should approach it as a serious athlete. You will maximize your ability to hit the ball, while playing injury-free, when you are in good general condition and have exercised the muscles which are important to golf. But if you ignore the beneficial role of fitness, you must play with a self-imposed handicap.

12
COURSE CONTROL

Course management means just what it says—how you manage your game from shot to shot as you maneuver the ball from the first tee to the 18th green. Golf is a constant decision-making process: On every shot you have to decide where the best place is to hit the ball and what the best route is to get it there. Then you have to follow up on that decision by making the swing that will produce the shot, and that's where the glitch comes in—every golfer knows from experience that the ball doesn't always go where he or she intends for it to go. Effective course management will help keep you out of "high-risk" trouble areas, which are the real score killers, when the shot is off target.

There are three factors that make up course management: knowing your game, knowing the course, and knowing the conditions. All are crucial; none is more important than the other.

It's good to have a warm hat when the cold winds blow at the British Open.

KNOWING YOUR GAME

It's pretty hard not to be familiar with certain characteristics of your own game. For example, it should be obvious to you whether you're a right-to-left or left-to-right player and whether you tend to hit the ball high or low. But do you know how far you hit each club? I mean *exactly* how far? Most amateurs know the approximate distance they get out of each club in their bag, while tour pros know *precisely.* If I hit a full pitching wedge from a good, flat lie under calm conditions, I know that it will go 118 yards. Not "about 115" or "almost 120," but precisely 118. Given the same conditions, my 9-iron goes 133 yards.

Of course, it's easier for a pro to know exactly how far his shots will go from club to club because he hits the ball solidly much more consistently than the casual player. So your best bet is to find out the average yardage you get with each club. Start with the sand wedge: hit 14 practice balls and pace off the distance of each (disregard the two longest and two shortest), calculating the average distance of the 10 remaining balls. Repeat with every club in the bag, including the driver.

You'll hit some shots a little more solidly than others, so the balls will end up near one another, but not all exactly the same distance. The mistake most amateurs make in club selection is that they always figure on hitting every shot perfectly, which in fact occurs only part of the time—even pros don't get "all of it" with every shot. So when you plan on hitting the shot perfectly but don't, it ends up short of the target. That's why amateurs underclub so often—not because they are incapable of hitting the ball the required distance with that particular club, but because they don't always hit it solidly enough to get the distance needed. Of course, there are going to be times when you do catch it sweet and the ball goes past the target, but it will average out in the long run.

Also, while checking your distances, find out how far your average carry is with the longer clubs—driver, fairway woods, and long irons. This information is invaluable when you have a hazard like water or sand that you can either lay up short of or try to get over.

KNOWING THE COURSE

It won't do you a whole lot of good to know how far you average with each club if you don't know how far away the target is. Most courses feature something to indicate the yardage to the middle of the green, be it a small bush or stake in the rough or a small marker embedded in the middle of the fairway. Some courses label sprinkler heads precisely to the yard; others list on the scorecard distances from specific landmarks.

Part of my caddy's job is to know the subtleties of the course and its yardages. When I get to my ball, I want to know the answers to any relevant yardage questions I may have, such as: How far is it to carry that creek in front of the green? How many yards to the very front of the green? How many to the pin? Again, you may be thinking precise yardages don't mean that much to you since you don't hit the ball as consistently as a pro. Maybe not, but simply knowing that you've done your homework and that you know "*exactly* how far" instead of "*about* how far" is a confidence booster.

If your home course doesn't have any kind of yardage indicators in the fairway, make it your business to do some pacing and compile your own. What you find may surprise you.

FAVORITE COURSES

Despite making my living as a touring pro, there are a lot of famous golf courses with wonderful reputations that I've yet to have the chance to play. But among the ones that I have been on, here are my top 10 favorites:

1. Pinehurst No. 2, Pinehurst, North Carolina
2. Colonial, Fort Worth, Texas
3. Winged Foot (West), Mamaroneck, New York
4. Harbour Town, Hilton Head, South Carolina
5. The Country Club, Brookline, Massachusetts
6. Pebble Beach, Pebble Beach, California
7. St. Andrews (Old), St. Andrews, Scotland
8. Southern Hills, Tulsa, Oklahoma
9. Riviera, Los Angeles, California
10. Augusta National, Augusta, Georgia

If you don't believe in the value of knowing yardages and would instead rather get a feel for the distance solely by sight, you're not alone. In the old days, golfers, even pros, rarely took the pains to find out exact yardages, and some old-timers today still scoff that they never had to go to such lengths. Maybe they didn't, but I don't agree that it's a waste of time—I see it as a way to improve your score by using your head. Jack Nicklaus was perhaps the first player to research extensively a course and its yardages, and no one can argue with Jack's success. That's not to say that it's the main reason for his outstanding record, but these days you won't find a tour pro who doesn't know the exact number of yards between his ball and the flag stick as he steps up to an approach.

KNOWING THE CONDITIONS

Be fully aware of all conditions affecting play. Find out about the speed of the greens before teeing off; whether the course is soft or firm; whether the rough is long or short. Check the wind before every shot for strength and direction so you have a clue how it will affect ball flight. Playing conditions will change from day to day, hour to hour, and shot to shot; being conscious of them is part of good course management.

TEE-TO-GREEN STRATEGY

Amateurs usually have tunnel vision when it comes to playing golf, aiming only for two things: the center of the fairway and the flag. However, it isn't that simple (at least if you want to score your best), and you should learn to determine the best part of the fairway to aim for, whether you're teeing off or laying up short of a green. You should also learn when it's safe to go for the pin and when you should play instead for the fat of the green.

Control Means Good Decision-Making

When people hear the word *control* in regard to golf, they usually think it means being conservative. I disagree. Being in control means making intelligent decisions—knowing when to be aggressive and when to be cautious. Loss of control is reflected in poor decision-making, such as trying to thread the needle of a very tight fairway with a driver instead of using less club or dunking an approach in water by shooting for a pin tucked close to a pond instead of aiming for the fat of the green.

Plan your strategy before teeing off to help stay "one jump ahead."

Look at it this way: you have direct control over your decision-making, but you don't have direct control over where the shot is going. You're human, not a machine, so bad shots are going to happen due to physical mistakes—they're simply unavoidable. What *is* avoidable are mental mistakes—or, in other words, poor decisions. Since the way the game is played varies from player to player, so will decision-making. You may decide to play a 150-yard approach shot into the wind differently from how I will. How decisions are made depends on your personality and the individual aspects of your game, but when it comes to tee-to-green play, it will simplify things to base your decision-making on one rule.

> Always play the ball to the spot that will set up the easiest next shot.

Sound simple? It is. Think of it as a checkers game, where you always want to stay one jump ahead of yourself. The same idea applies to golf. From the tee, I want to aim the ball for that part of the fairway that will offer me the best combination of a flat lie and favorable angle from which to approach the green. That may indeed turn out to be the center of the fairway, but often an architect will put it more toward the left or right side, perhaps next to a bunker or pond. Pins are often placed close to the edge of the green, guarded by sand, water, or a drop-off in land. In either case, a shot that misses its target, even if only by a little, can end up in trouble. It's up to you to decide when to take the risk and when to play it safe. To win at golf you've got to have both the guts and patience of a race-car driver. You have to wait for your opportunities to score and then go hard after them when they arise, but you also have to know when to ease up on the gas. Driving at one extreme or the other usually won't earn you the checkered flag: if you floor it constantly you're likely to crash, and if you're too cautious you'll finish the race, but somewhere back in the pack.

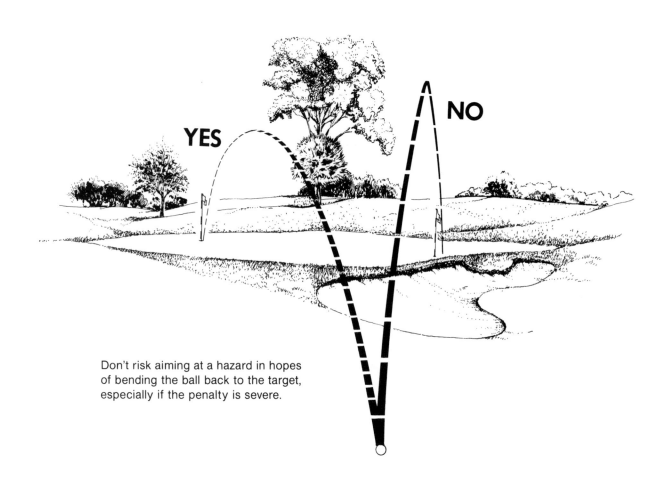

Don't risk aiming at a hazard in hopes of bending the ball back to the target, especially if the penalty is severe.

When to Be Aggressive, When to Be Cautious

Exactly when you decide to be aggressive and when to exercise caution should depend on: 1. your personality; 2. how well you're striking the ball at that particular time; 3. how the individual characteristics of your game fit the particular hole being played; and 4. the situation in which you find yourself.

1. *Personality*

If you are naturally an expressive, full-tilt type of person, you'll gravitate toward an aggressive playing style. Players who come to mind are Walter Hagen, Arnold Palmer, Greg Norman, and Seve Ballesteros. If you're more laid back you'll probably be less comfortable taking a lot of big risks.

2. *Ball-Striking*

Aggression should depend partly on how well you're playing. Very simply, if I'm confident about my ball-striking and my shots are going where I want them to, I'll be more likely to try to hit a narrow fairway with my driver, or shoot at a well-guarded pin. Conversely, if I'm not hitting the ball particularly well from tee to green, I'll back off and try mainly to keep the ball in play.

3. *How Your Game Fits the Hole*

If your natural shot allows you to aim away from trouble and work the ball back toward the pin, then it lends itself toward being aggressive and trying to put the ball close. My natural shot is a slight fade, so I'll be more aggressive when trouble is to the right of my target, allowing me to aim away from it. If the shot behaves the way I want it to, it will be on target; if it flies relatively straight, I'll still be out of trouble. Most pros will not aim directly at a hazard (at least not an unforgiving one such as water) and try to curve the ball away from it, since the risk of penalty is just too big.

4. *Situation*

As far as situation is concerned, I think it's pretty obvious when the position you're in dictates aggressive or conservative play. If I'm standing in the final fairway trailing by one, I'll attack the pin, no matter how well it's guarded or how I happen to be striking the ball. If I'm in the same place with a two-shot lead, I'll aim away from trouble and for the middle of the green.

Take the 1988 Independent Insurance Agents Open, as an example. I reached the final hole trailing Greg Norman, my playing partner, by a stroke. The hole, the 18th at the Tournament Players Course at the Woodlands, is a long par four with a pond butting sharply against the front of the green. That day the pin was cut close to the front edge near the water, so shooting for it was a definite risk. Greg made the smart play with his approach, hitting the club that would carry his ball easily over the water and onto the rear half of the green. With a stroke to make up, the situation forced me to go for the flag. The yardage called for a 3-iron. If I didn't need birdie, I would have hit a 2-iron instead to keep away from the pond. I made solid contact

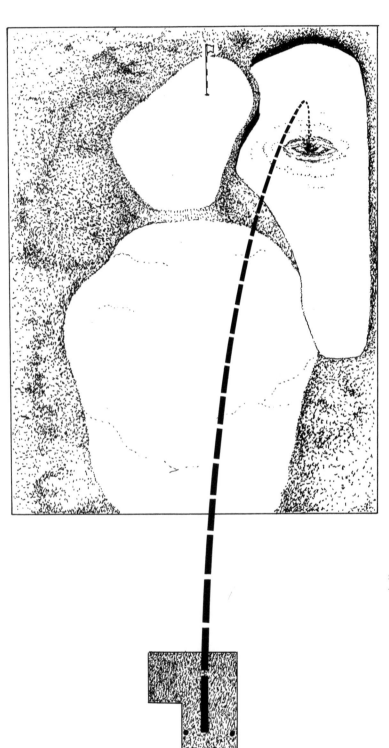

Let pin placement shape your approach strategy: attack the flag when it's out in the open, but back down when the hole is tightly guarded.

and the shot finished four feet from the hole. Greg two-putted. Then I sank mine to send it into sudden death, which I won with a birdie on the fourth extra hole—which happened to be the 18th.

Don't Be Afraid to Be Patient

I sometimes think amateurs don't use enough patience on the course because they're afraid they aren't playing the game hard enough or as it was meant to be played. Part of the problem may have to do with the fact that Palmer did so much to glamorize aggressive golf with his many head-on collisions with golf courses during his heyday in the '60s. The thought of playing safe rarely occurred to Arnold—he was always trying to get to the green from wherever he happened to find the ball, whether it was the middle of the fairway or the middle of the woods. It was exciting to watch, and he won a lot of tournaments that way, but when you live by the sword you die by the sword, as two of Arnold's own U.S. Open experiences proved: he won in 1960 at Cherry Hills by firing a final-round 65; he lost the 1964 Open at Olympic in an 18-hole play-off with Billy Casper after wasting a seven-shot lead with nine holes to play in the last round. Hindsight is 20/20, but knowing Arnie, he would play it the same way if he had it to do over again.

Tee-Shot Strategy

I couldn't include a chapter on course management without having a specific section on the tee shot, since it's the most crucial shot on every hole. Miss the fairway (or green on par threes) and you're immediately in a scrambling position, having to recover from rough, sand, woods, or worse. I'm not considered a long hitter by tour standards, but I'm usually among the top 10 in accuracy off the tee, and that's a stat that's important to me, because I'd rather be straight than long. Most amateurs are enthralled with distance, and they are always looking for ways to add extra yardage to their drives. I believe that if the average player worked more on hitting a few more fairways per round instead of hitting the ball a few more yards, he or she would score better.

One way to hit more fairways and greens is to concentrate on the shot at the tee. Remember that the teeing area is not confined to the thin line between the markers, but instead is a box extending two club lengths deep—an important difference on par threes when two club lengths can mean the difference between a three-footer for birdie and a 10-footer.

Tee the ball toward the side of the box that's consistent with the direction you're intending to bend the ball. For a draw, tee to the left side; for a fade, tee to the right. Only the ball has to be within the boundaries of the tee box—it's perfectly legal to take your address with one or both feet outside. Although I play by this rule, I will break it if there's something about the "correct" side of the tee that I don't particularly like—perhaps it's on a slight slope (not every teeing area is perfectly flat) or the turf is torn up. If there's something about the area that makes me uncomfortable, I'll search out a spot that I like, even if it's on the "wrong" side.

Don't take for granted that the tee markers are lined up to point you down the fairway, since they get moved around from day to day so the turf gets equal wear, and sometimes they are replaced unevenly. That's one reason why I disregard the markers (except to make sure the ball is teed behind them) and pick an intermediate target a couple of feet in front of the ball to aim over.

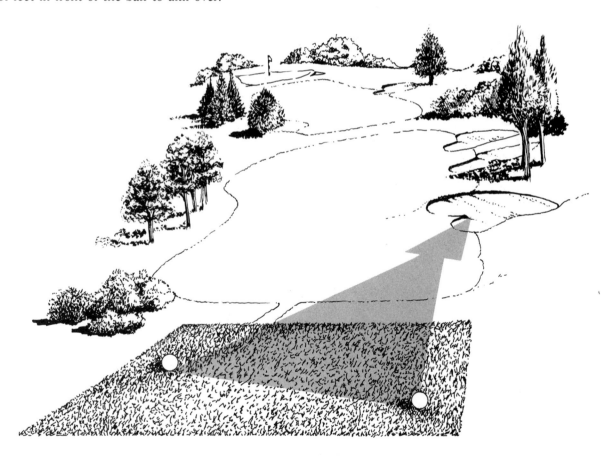

Don't trust that the tee markers will point you straight down the fairway. Careless placement of one or the other could inadvertently steer you away from your target.

The rules of golf require that only the ball be placed between the tee markers—it's perfectly legal for the player to stand outside of them.

Because the tee markers are frequently moved, the yardage to the middle of the green will vary on par threes. The tees on most short holes feature some kind of marker that reflects exactly the yardage listed on the card, so always take a second to pace off the distance between the permanent marker and the tee markers and add or subtract the difference to get the exact number, since it may have an influence on club selection.

METAL WOODS

Metal woods began appearing on tour in the early 1980s, and in my opinion they're an equipment innovation that's here to stay. The chief difference between wooden woods and metal woods (besides the material they're made of) is that wooden heads are solid masses, while metal heads are actually hollow shells, usually filled with a light material such as Styrofoam. Because nearly all the weight of the metal head is concentrated in this outer shell, mishits go straighter than with a wooden club—an excellent reason for the recreational player to play them, especially off the tee. But metal isn't for everyone. Even though my tastes in golf are pretty traditional, I made the switch to metal woods in 1983, since I feel the advantages they offer are too great to ignore.

13
SELF-CONTROL

Whenever I see someone get angry at himself on the golf course, I have to admit that I admire him for it. That's because I'm the same way: I've always had pretty high self-expectations, and I tend to get disgusted when I don't meet them. Good competitors often get angry at themselves, but they don't let that anger affect their performance. I progressed from being a hotheaded kid to a self-controlled tournament player. Along the way I learned to channel the negative feelings produced by a bad hole or a poor shot into bearing down on the remainder of the round. I wouldn't have achieved what I have so far if I hadn't made this adjustment.

Golf is 90% mental.

The saying that golf is 90 percent mental applies here, meaning that not only do you have to think your way around the course, but you have to keep a handle on your emotions so that they don't interfere with your ability to make smart decisions. That can be difficult, since there's so much downtime in golf, giving you plenty of opportunity to scold yourself for hitting a horrible shot as you search for the ball in the woods or berate yourself for missing that three-footer as your playing partners hole out. The fact that golf is such an individual game also leaves only yourself to blame when things go sour, unless you happen to get a bad break.

One of the great things about golf is that every shot is a different challenge—rarely do you face the exact same shot twice. Some are easier than others, and you have to take that into account and give yourself a break when facing tough circumstances. Here's an example: In the 1988 Open on the final day I was a shot ahead of Nick Faldo, with whom I was playing, when we reached the 17th green. I had a birdie putt about 15 feet long that was downhill and very fast. I knew that it was the kind of putt that, if it didn't go in, was going to run at least a few feet past the cup. I studied it well, then tapped the ball just hard enough to get it rolling, but it slid by the cup and

Taking time out at the British Open for a baked potato.

stopped a full six feet below. I wasn't pleased at that, but I honestly couldn't get upset with myself about it because I simply couldn't have hit it any softer—circumstances simply dictated that I either made it or had a tester coming back. As it turned out, I missed the comebacker and dropped back into a tie with Faldo. Then I had to scramble for a tying par on 18.

Note that I'm not saying that I don't get down on myself at all on the course—I certainly do. Let's face it: anyone who has played much golf knows that it's pretty easy to get a little ticked off at yourself at some point during the course of a round. That's because perfection does not lend itself to the game, yet that's what we're constantly striving for—to hit every fairway, stick every approach close, hole every putt. That might sound like fun, but it would probably get pretty dull after a while. However, I don't think anyone will ever be able to attain that kind of perfection on the golf course, because we just cannot strike perfectly every drive, iron, pitch, chip, and putt.

I don't get angry about physical mistakes—say, a pushed drive or pulled iron (unless it happens several times in a row)—because, as I said, I'm not a machine, and I realize that it's going to happen from time to time. What I *do* get upset about are mental mistakes, because they *can* be (or should be) prevented. But even if a mental mistake does occur and does cost you a stroke, you're only cheating yourself if you let it bother you enough to interfere with how you play the next shot. Instead, use the extra adrenaline it creates to bear down and fight back. Take the first round of the 1989 Players Championship. I was playing pretty well and had gotten it to three under when I hooked my tee shot into a large fairway trap on 14, a medium-length par four. To get to the green from there required cheating close to some trees that lined the fairway on the left side. I decided it was worth the risk, since I'd been playing pretty well, but I pulled the ball left, it ricocheted hard off a branch and flew even farther left, landing in dense woods and undergrowth. It didn't turn up after five minutes of searching, so I had to go back and drop another ball in the trap. This time I laid up short of the green, then pitched on and two-putted for a triple-bogey seven—back to even par. When I got to the next tee, I was steaming; I still couldn't believe I had been dumb enough to go for the green from that trap! But instead of dwelling on the disaster, I just decided there was no way I was going to finish at even or above par, then proceeded to go par-eagle-birdie-birdie for a four-under 68.

THE VALUE OF GRINDING

When I won at Oak Hill, I shot 71-64-73-70. Which round do you think won it for me? My answer wouldn't be the 64. Believe it or not, if any round won the tournament for me, it was the 73 on Saturday. Why? Because I wasn't hitting the ball well at all that day and could easily have shot 77 or 78. But I worked like a dog that day to get the ball up and down and save as many strokes as I could (I hit only eight greens), and though I wasn't particularly happy shooting three over par, I was still somewhat proud because I knew it easily could have been higher. That 73 took a lot more work than the 64.

Think back to your own experiences. The most satisfying pars you've ever made probably weren't when you hit the green in regulation and two-putted. The ones that most likely stick out are the scrambling ones, when you had to punch the ball out of the woods, pitch on, and sink a 10-footer to save four. Some days golf seems easy; your swing is smooth and controlled and the putter feels good in your hands. It takes a lot more work on the days when the shots often aren't going where you want them and you've got to rely on your short game to salvage your score. It also takes a lot of guts and determination, since it's mentally taxing to rely continually on pitches, chips, sand shots, and putting to save yourself, but it's a fact of golfing life that you're going to have days like that. Even professionals rarely go four rounds without having an off day, and what you do on that day can mean the difference between winning and losing. Scratching out a 72 that easily might have been 75 can mean the difference between first place and fifth place.

Although the average amateur doesn't play that many four-round tournaments, he or she will still benefit from this kind of attitude. Don't give in to bogey so easily if you miss a green—get into the idea of grinding and make up your mind that you're going to fight that hole to the finish. I really believe you have to have something of a mean streak in you to win at golf, and mine comes out especially when I feel as if the course is taking a few cuffs at me, and the only way I can get back at it is to bear down and save pars and make birdies.

PSYCHE YOURSELF UP, DON'T PSYCHE YOURSELF OUT

There's no doubt that pressure makes any golf shot a little tougher to perform—sometimes a lot tougher. A three-footer for par may not be much of a strain during a casual round, but the same putt with the club championship riding on it won't be such a breeze. Every player feels the heat in a pressure situation. Don't get the idea that pros don't feel it—heck, I get as nervous as anybody when it comes down to a single shot that makes the difference between winning or losing. When I face a "must" shot, I try to concentrate on psyching myself up, where most amateurs make the mistake of psyching themselves out, mainly by dwelling on the consequences of failing to succeed at pulling off the needed shot. Players who are good at handling pressure try to crowd their minds with the opposite kinds of thoughts: visualizing the shot going where they want it to and concentrating on what they have to do to get it there. I know that's easier said than done, but it's true.

One thing I know from experience is that the more times you play in pressure situations, the more you'll improve at performing in them. Knowing that you've been there before is a confidence-booster. That's why I recommend that, if you like to compete in tournaments, you play in a lot of them—the more practice you get at playing under pressure, the better you'll get at it. One of the most high-pressure situations any pro faces is when he tries to earn his tour card. The first time I attempted it, I bogeyed the final three holes to miss qualifying by a stroke. The next time I tried, I nailed it, and, believe me, having been through the experience once already was a big help in being successful the second time. Just knowing that you've been there before makes you psychologically stronger.

The more practice you get at playing under pressure, the better you get at it.

DEVELOP A PRESHOT ROUTINE

Your ability to shut out extraneous thoughts and focus on the task at hand will be aided by using a preshot routine. There isn't a pro who doesn't recognize the value of such a routine and who doesn't use one. I don't think of my shot as starting at the precise moment when the clubhead makes contact with the ball. The shot begins as I pull the club out of the bag, because that's when I start to visualize, or imagine, the shot I want to hit. I imagine the motion of the swing, the feel of the club against the ball, the image of the ball against the sky as it curves gently toward the target and lands there. Then I pick out an intermediate target a few feet in front of the ball—maybe a leaf or spot on the ground—and take my address, aiming the clubface directly at the intermediate target. Then I check my target, waggle the clubhead back with my hands and arms to loosen them up, check the target one more time, then start my takeaway.

You'll find that going through the same set of actions before every shot will help you shut out any distracting thoughts, noises, and objects. When I'm through with my routine and am ready to pull the trigger, the only thing on my mind is the shot I want to hit and a swing key or two that will help me hit it. At that second, the possibility of failure is the *furthest* thing from my mind.

My preshot routine begins when I pull the club out of my bag. While doing this I'm busy forming a picture in my mind of the shot I want to hit.

I always pick out an intermediate target (here signified by the second ball) a couple of feet in front of the ball to align the clubface with.

Then I line up my body alignment in relation to the clubface.

Once I'm comfortably over the ball, I check my primary target . . .

. . . waggle the clubhead back to loosen my wrists and forearms . . .

. . . rest the clubhead briefly behind the ball . . .

. . . then start the takeaway.

14
GIVING YOUR ALL IN MATCH OR MEDAL PLAY

The most popular form of competition among amateurs is a friendly form of match play among regular playing partners, either four-ball or individual. Still, you're bound to compete in a stroke-play event (also known as medal play) from time to time, so following are tips for doing your best in either format.

As a touring pro, I've had more experience at stroke play than with any other form of competition. The obvious difference between stroke and match play is that in match play you can afford to take more chances, since all you have to lose is the particular hole you're playing—total score means nothing. If I'm playing a match, I don't care if I shoot 80 as long as I win more holes than my opponent.

In stroke play, you have to keep the big picture—your final score—in mind at all times, which means weighing your risks much more carefully, since a poor hole is something you have to live with, and it may well come back to haunt you. Because of this most players will, on the average, play more conservatively in stroke play, especially when it comes to getting out of trouble. In stroke play I'll almost never force a low-percentage shot out of a tight spot in an effort to

Leaving the final green after finishing the U.S. Open with Nick Faldo at The Country Club in 1988.

save par if it could just as easily result in a double or triple bogey. The only time I'll throw all caution aside in stroke play is if I have to make up ground in order to catch up to the leader toward the end of the final day.

One of the reasons I've enjoyed playing on the Ryder Cup team is because the format is match play, both team and individual—something we pros on tour don't see much of anymore. As a competitive person, I really like going head to head against another person or team.

I definitely am more willing to take risks in match play, but only if the actions of my opponent force me to. If it strongly appears that he's going to beat me on the hole, I'll take a chance—even a big one—to get back into it, but only if I'm reasonably sure I'll lose the hole if I don't. A typical example is on the greens. If I'm facing a 40-footer to halve the hole, I'm not worried about lagging the ball close for a two-putt; I just want to do the best I can to get it into the hole, so you can bet the ball won't be short of the cup. If it misses and goes five feet past, I don't care, since the next putt doesn't matter. However, if I have to get down in two from 40 feet to tie, my main concern is to get the approach putt close enough to tap in. If it happens to drop, that's great, but the last thing I want to do is run the ball well past and end up three-putting to lose the hole.

Another good reason for taking a gamble when the chips are down is because not only can it get you back into the hole, but it will be a psychological punch to your opponent, while giving you a lift. If the risk doesn't work out, it's no loss since the hole was in jeopardy anyway. Be sure, however, that your opponent definitely has the upper hand before trying a chancy shot, since the possibility still exists that he may get into trouble. Just because a player has a relatively easy approach doesn't mean he'll hit the green. And just because he's hit the green doesn't guarantee par. What I mean is, don't bet the farm until you're sure you have to.

YOU VS. YOUR OPPONENT, YOUR OPPONENT VS. YOU

In a stroke-play tournament, I concentrate solely on my own game without paying any attention to how my playing partners are scoring. In match play, though, I want to be fully aware of what my opponent is up to at all times, because it can influence whether I play a particular shot aggressively or cautiously.

You, in turn, have an influence on your opponent, and the best advice I can give you to put the pressure on is to keep the ball in play. I like nothing better than to tee off first and put the ball in the fairway, then step back and let my opponent make the next move. The same goes for approach shots and even putting. On the green I like the security of being first in, putting the pressure on the other guy to match me. For example, if both my opponent and I are facing long putts for birdie, and I go first and leave mine four or five feet short, I'll usually go ahead and putt out rather than mark and wait. (Although the rules of golf state that the player farthest from the hole should play first, it's okay to putt out if your partner gives you permission.) That's because if I mark it, he knows that I have a missable putt left, and that lets him relax a little psychologically. But if he gets his hopes up just a little that I might miss and I sink it instead, it turns out to be a slight blow to him. The obvious risk here is that if I miss the par putt, the heat is off him and all he has to do is two-putt to win. But it's a chance I'll usually take in match play.

Along these same lines runs an old match-play philosophy that recommends keeping your tee shot a little shorter than your opponent's, giving you the opportunity to hit the green first with the approach, putting pressure on your foe. I don't buy this way of thinking because the door can easily swing both ways—if you miss the green instead, you take the pressure off him.

You have an influence on your opponent: to keep the pressure on, keep the ball in play.

TEAM PLAY

Two-man best-ball competitions allow you even more room to take risks and play aggressively, since you have a partner to fall back on in case you find trouble. Again, temper your gambles according to your partner's position and what your opponents are up to. (Remember, though, that this doesn't mean you should take foolish risks just because your partner's ball is safe.)

It's good strategy for the more accurate player to tee off first, since if he hits the fairway it takes the pressure off his partner. If player one happens to hit an errant shot, his partner can then be more conservative in an effort to keep the ball in play.

The place where teamwork can really pay off, though, is on the greens. The rules of golf state that the ball lying farthest from the hole should be played first. In team play, however, if it's one member's turn to play, he can allow his teammate to play before him, even if the teammate's ball is closer to the hole. So if I have a 20-footer for birdie and my partner has a five-footer for par, it's our option to let him putt first. Should he sink it, I can go for the birdie without fear of three-putting, since our team has already chalked up a par.

Another way a teammate can be of help on the greens is by showing his partner the line, or break, of a putt. Suppose my partner has 10 feet for double bogey, while I have a 12-footer for birdie along the same line. Instead of telling him to pick it up, since he's out of the hole, I'll ask him to putt it first and go to school on it. I'll do this even if I'm sure of which direction a putt will move, since it can only help reinforce in my mind the way I want to play my putt.

SCORER'S TENT

That tent you see players briefly disappearing into following each round at a professional tournament is the scorer's tent. There, each player checks his scorecard (kept by a playing partner), then signs it. His signature, along with the signature of the scorer, makes the score official; and he is responsible for securing both signatures.

In the event that one or more of the individual hole scores is incorrect, the penalty depends on whether the actual score for the hole(s) was higher or lower than that indicated on the card. If the actual score was lower, the player must accept whatever amount the card reads. If, however, the actual score is higher than the number on the card, the player is disqualified.

Keeping and signing for a correct score and showing up on time for tee-off are the two most important responsibilities a player has. To prevent any scoring mistakes, I always keep my own score, and so does my caddy. After the round I check my card against his and also against the card that the volunteer scorer has kept. (A volunteer scorer walks with every group.) After that I check it against the card my playing partner has kept, and when I'm sure everything is correct I sign it.

15
LIFE ON TOUR

I play in about 30 tournaments per year (six to eight overseas), the bulk of them falling between the months of January and August. Most of my schedule is planned out well in advance, with Sarah and me taking care of the travel and lodging arrangements. I prefer it this way, since 13 years on tour have made me familiar enough with each tour stop to know the best places to stay and where to get a decent steak. Here's what a typical week looks like.

Having a postround chat with Greg Norman at the 1988 World Series of Golf, Firestone Country Club.

Monday

Most of my Mondays between January and October are spent appearing at corporate outings, of which I attend about 20 per year. Typically, I start the morning by giving a clinic for 45 minutes to an hour, mainly trying to explain and demonstrate my swing method in simple terms. After that, everybody hits the course, and I bounce from group to group and play a few holes with everybody. Following the round, everybody gathers again for refreshments, and sometimes dinner before the day comes to an end. The location of the particular outing may or may not be close to where that week's tournament is being played, so I may end up on a plane that night or the next morning to get where I have to go.

Tuesday

My main focus on Tuesday is to get situated in town and to get to the practice tee to do any work on my swing that I think needs to be done. Then I'll get some practice time in on the course, sometimes only nine holes instead of a full 18, since I'm pretty familiar with most of the tournament courses we play.

1989: Holding the U.S. Open
trophy again a year later at
Oak Hill.

Wednesday

Wednesday is pro-am day, so if the tournament holds one (most of them do), I have to play in it. I usually request a morning tee time, leaving the afternoon free for practice. I really consider playing in the pro-am important, since it's the last time I'll get to see the course before the actual tournament starts and because each pro has to post a score. Not only that, but it helps charity. My main priority Wednesday evening is spending the evening quietly. Usually I'll relax by watching TV or maybe seeing a movie; then I go to bed at a decent hour so I can feel 100 percent when I tee off on Thursday.

Thursday

The first round of the tournament. Thursday night is also spent quietly, to conserve energy for Friday. In bed, after lights are out, I'll take a few minutes to review the day's round and imagine ways to improve for Friday's performance before going to sleep.

Friday

The second round. If I had a morning tee time on Thursday, then Friday's will be in the afternoon; and vice versa. If I make the cut, that evening will also be spent quietly, capped off with a mental replay of what happened that day. If I miss the cut, it's home for the weekend.

Saturday and Sunday

Obviously, Saturdays and Sundays are more fun for a player if he's in contention. If I'm not around the lead, however, and there doesn't seem to be much chance that I'll get near it, I still play hard—for a couple of reasons. One, it may be valuable experience if I happen to end up in contention at that particular tournament the following year. Two, now that I've gained some notoriety as a pretty good player, people follow and watch even when I'm not in the thick of things, so I always try to give them their money's worth.

If I should happen to be in or near the lead after Saturday's round, it means I'll be among the last to tee off on Sunday. Despite that, I make it a point to get up fairly early instead of lazing in bed. After a good breakfast I make sure to keep busy (usually by reading the Sunday paper) to avoid speculating on what may happen that afternoon. Ideally I'll get to the course about an hour before teeing

THE CUT
What exactly is "the cut"? It's when the tournament field is cut approximately in half, almost always after the second round. The low-70 scorers, plus those who've tied for the 70th place, qualify to stick around for the final two rounds and are guaranteed to get paid. The rest have to make early arrangements to go home.

off, giving me plenty of time to loosen up and hit some putts. I don't want to make the mistake of getting to the course too early, though, since waiting around too much breeds anxiety and tension. That's because I still get nervous when I'm in position to win, which shows I really care.

HOME SCHEDULE

If I happen to take a week off, I normally won't touch a golf club for the first few days but instead simply relax by spending time with Sarah and the kids and doing a little fishing with friends. Home is the perfect place to get away from the rigors and pressures of the tour, since everyone I know there treats me as a normal person, not a celebrity—which is something I really appreciate.

On Thursday, I'll hit 50 or 60 balls on the practice range; that's all. On Friday I'll do the same thing and also get in some practice putting. Not until Saturday and Sunday will I go out to practice on the course, but when I do, I'll play four or five balls so I can hit a wide variety of shots. I'll also spend some time off the course hitting chips, pitches, and sand shots. Then I'm usually back on the road that Sunday night or Monday morning.

CADDIES

Tour caddies have to do a lot more than tote a bag of clubs around. The four most important things I expect of my caddy are:

1. Be on time. Whether it's for a practice round or tournament round, no pro wants to be waiting around for his caddy to show up.
2. Know the yardages. When I get to the ball I expect quick, accurate answers to any questions I have concerning distance. Most caddies keep their own yardage books on specific courses; if the tournament is going to be at a site unfamiliar to the pro, it's up to the caddy to get there early and do some homework.
3. Supply sound advice on club selection. But *only* when I ask for it.
4. Quiet the gallery. A good caddy should always keep an eye on the crowd to watch for potential disturbances—movement or noise—that could distract his player and politely ask the fans to stay still while the shot is made.

VOLUNTEERS

No professional tournament could ever take place without the participation of the hundreds of volunteers who generously give their time to work the gates, concessions, and scoreboards and as marshals, standard bearers, and scorers. Although many pros march grimly from Thursday through Sunday wearing their game faces, that's not to imply that we don't appreciate the many folks (there may be from 1,500 to 2,500 volunteers working a given tournament) out there helping to make it happen, because we do. There isn't a pro who doesn't realize that a tournament couldn't take place without them.

Showing off a white marlin caught off Oregon Inlet, North Carolina. (left to right) Me, Robert St. Clair, David Bryne, and John Bryant.

Throughout most of my career I've preferred to use several different caddies during the course of each season, but in 1989 I stuck with one guy, Greg Rita. Greg and I go back to the 1983 Hartford Open, which I won. Since then I've hired him a number of times to work different tournaments. In 1988 he caddied for me at four events, two of which I won—the U.S. Open and the Nabisco Championship.

Most of the caddies who've worked for me know that I don't need any cheerleading out there; I'm the type of player who would rather concentrate on his game instead of making small talk between shots. I also like making all my own green-reading decisions.

Any caddy who's ever worked for me also knows not to break out any balls with number four on them during competition—a superstition of mine. (Why? Because I make bogeys with them.)

The caddies have come a long way in recent years to organize themselves as a group and upgrade their image. They have their own organization now, the dues of which go toward funding a mobile home that travels to each tour site. There, meals are cooked and sold at a good price, giving them a place to eat and gather when they have spare time during the day. The organization has also made it possible for some of the caddies to get paid for wearing certain logos on their visors during televised tournaments.

THE MEDIA

A chapter on tour life wouldn't be complete without mentioning the media—magazines, newspapers, radio, and TV. The media are our only true contacts with the public, so I like to do all I can to cooperate with them. Its unfortunate, however, that the only impression many people, including the media, get of the players is that during competition. Some players come across as pretty stern when playing; this usually isn't a true reflection of what most of the guys are like when they're off the course. Think of it this way: an executive wouldn't joke around during an important decision-making meeting; he or she would have his or her mind on the business at hand. So does the tournament golfer.

The members of the media congregate in the tournament media center (formerly known as the pressroom). There they're provided with table space, typewriters, televisions, telephones, and fax machines. At the front of the room a large scoreboard is set up so everyone can stay abreast of up-to-the-minute score changes without leaving the area.

The media center also features an interview room or area, where reporters can gather as a group to quiz a particular player with any questions they have. (Usually there's a small stage and microphone up front where the player sits and speaks.) Commonly, the previous week's winner meets with the media on Tuesday or Wednesday. Then, as the tournament progresses from Thursday through Sunday, the leaders after each round (and eventually the winner) are requested to appear. I say "requested" because players have the option to decline an interview, though nearly all comply, although sometimes it's easier than others. It's obviously fun to go for an interview on Sunday night if you happen to have won the tournament and a lot tougher if you've narrowly lost.

WHY THE GAME'S STILL FUN FOR ME

Why wouldn't golf be fun for me? you might wonder. Well, when you play five or six rounds per week, up to 40 weeks per year, there are days when you get up and really don't feel like playing. There are plenty of players who've been out on tour for a number of years who have lost the desire and enthusiasm they once had. Although playing the tour appears glamorous, tour life has its down side: a lot of time is spent away from home and family, and the constant travel can get very tiresome. It's easy to get disheartened when your game goes sour; this applies especially to young players who are still trying to prove themselves and scratch out a living, and it's even true of veterans.

The main thing that keeps me going is that I still feel as if I have yet to reach my full potential as a player—there's still room for

Meeting the press at the 1989 PGA Championship.

improvement in my game. Part of that has to do with my nature. I'm the kind of person who's pretty difficult to please; a real perfectionist. So the challenge of always improving is part of why I'm still enthusiastic about the game. Besides that, practically every facet of golf fascinates me: studying the swing; the mental side; equipment; course architecture, history—there are so many elements to the game that it's hard to get bored with it.

Another reason I continue to enjoy golf is because the feeling of hitting a good, solid, accurate shot, whether a drive or a putt, is still wonderful to me and has been since I first started playing. (Anyone who's ever played and fallen in love with the game, no matter what level he or she plays at, knows what I mean by that.) That's why I really like to practice and hit balls.

Finally, I'm an outdoorsman at heart, and since golf is played outside on some of the most beautiful parts of the earth (e.g., Pebble Beach), that becomes another reason why I'll never get tired of it.

Hopefully, you'll never reach the point where golf isn't fun anymore. Sure, there may be days when you get a little tired of it, but if you consistently find that you aren't enjoying yourself on the golf course, take some time to examine the reasons why you're out there. In Chapter 13 I said I admired people who got angry at themselves if their performance wasn't up to what they expected, but I don't mean *too* angry. If you aren't trying to earn a living by playing, believe me, it isn't worth getting that steamed up. Remember that golf is a game meant for recreation. Competition is only part of the reason you're out there; you're also there for the fresh air, exercise, the camaraderie of friends, and, of course, the feeling you get when you hit a well-struck shot. The day will come when my competitive days are behind me, and I know that I'll still love golf for all those reasons.

TOURNAMENT RECORD AND ACHIEVEMENTS

1970 Virginia State Junior

1972 Virginia State Junior

1973 Southeastern Amateur

1974 NCAA individual champion
Western Amateur
College Player of the Year
World Amateur Cup team

1975 Eastern Amateur
Walker Cup team
Virginia State Amateur
North and South Amateur

1976 North and South Amateur
Virginia State Amateur

1979 Pensacola Open

1980 Michelob-Houston Open
Manufacturers Hanover
   Westchester Classic

1983 Sammy Davis, Jr.-Greater Hartford
   Open
Ryder Cup team

1984 LaJet Classic

1985 Honda Classic
Panasonic-Las Vegas Invitational
Canadian Open
Ryder Cup team
Nissan Cup team
Arnold Palmer Award (PGA leading
   money winner)
Golf Writers Player of the Year

1986 Houston Open
Kirin Cup winning team

1987 Canadian Open
Federal Express-St. Jude Classic
NEC World Series of Golf
Dunhill Cup team (shot record 62
   at Old Course, St. Andrews)
Kirin Cup team
Golf Writers Player of the Year
Arnold Palmer Award

1988 Sanctuary Cove Classic (Australia)
Independent Insurance Agent
   Open
Memorial Tournament
United States Open
Nabisco Championships
Kirin Cup winning team
Arnold Palmer Award
Golf Writers Player of the Year
PGA Player of the Year

1989 Palm Meadows Cup (Australia)
United States Open
RMCC Invitational (team victory
   with Mark O'Meara)
Ryder Cup team
Dunhill Cup winning team
Kirin Cup winning team
Skins Game (top money winner)

INDEX